FROM IDEA TO ENTERPRISE

Comprehensive Blueprint for starting your own Business
Author: B Pily

TABLE OF CONTENTS

Sl. No	Content	Page
	Preface	4
	About the Author	6
	Introduction	7
A	Nurturing Ideas into Innovation	10
B	Navigating the Market Landscape	14
C	Charting Your Course	18
D	Securing Funding	23
E	Choosing the Right Legal Structure	27
F	Navigating Financing Options	31
G	Choosing the Right Location and Infrastructure	35
H	Building Your Brand	39
I	Launching Your Business	43
J	Operation Management	46
K	Legal and Regulatory Compliance	68
L	Focus on Customer Service	96
M	Manage Finances Effectively	99
N	Cultivate a Supportive Network	104
O	Human Resources and Team Building	107
P	Technology and IT Infrastructure	113
Q	Supply Chain Management	116
R	Customer Relationship Management	119
S	Conclusion	122

PREFACE

Welcome to "From Idea to Enterprise: Comprehensive Blueprint for Starting Your Own Business." This book is the culmination of my passion for entrepreneurship and my desire to share valuable insights and strategies with aspiring business owners like yourself.

Starting a business from scratch is an exhilarating journey filled with excitement, challenges, and opportunities. It's a journey that I've embarked on numerous times throughout my career, and I've learned invaluable lessons along the way. With this book, I aim to distill those lessons into a comprehensive guide that will help you navigate the complexities of entrepreneurship and build a successful enterprise.

"From Idea to Enterprise" is designed to be a practical roadmap for aspiring entrepreneurs at every stage of their journey. Whether you're in the early stages of brainstorming business ideas or you're preparing to launch your startup, this book provides actionable strategies, expert advice, and real-world examples to guide you through the process.

In these pages, you'll learn how to nurture your ideas into innovative concepts, secure funding for your venture, navigate legal and regulatory requirements, and cultivate a supportive network of mentors and peers. You'll also discover essential techniques for managing finances effectively, delivering exceptional customer service, and leveraging technology to drive business growth.

Throughout the book, I'll share personal anecdotes, insights from successful entrepreneurs, and practical exercises to help you apply the concepts to your own business journey. Whether you're dreaming of launching the next tech startup or opening a small retail store in your neighborhood, the principles and strategies outlined in this book are universally applicable to entrepreneurs in any industry or sector.

I believe that entrepreneurship is not just about building successful businesses—it's about making a positive impact on the world and creating opportunities for yourself and others. By sharing the knowledge and experiences contained within these pages, my hope is that you'll be inspired to pursue your entrepreneurial dreams with confidence, resilience, and determination.

Thank you for joining me on this journey. I wish you every success in your entrepreneurial endeavors, and I look forward to seeing your ideas come to life.

Warm regards,

B. Pily

About the Author

B. Pily is an entrepreneur, business strategist, and author dedicated to empowering aspiring entrepreneurs to turn their business dreams into reality. With a passion for innovation and a wealth of experience in the business world, B. Pily shares practical insights, actionable strategies, and expert advice to help individuals navigate the journey of entrepreneurship with confidence and clarity.

Having embarked on numerous entrepreneurial ventures throughout their career, B. Pily understands the challenges and opportunities that come with starting and growing a business from scratch. With a focus on creativity, resilience, and strategic thinking, B. Pily's approach to entrepreneurship emphasizes the importance of continuous learning, adaptation, and forward-thinking in today's dynamic business landscape.

Through their writing and speaking engagements, B. Pily inspires and motivates aspiring entrepreneurs to embrace their entrepreneurial spirit, overcome obstacles, and build successful enterprises that make a positive impact on the world. Whether you're a budding entrepreneur or a seasoned business owner, B. Pily's insights and expertise offer invaluable guidance on the path to entrepreneurial success.

Introduction:

The allure of entrepreneurship beckons many—a siren call promising freedom, fulfillment, and the opportunity to leave an indelible mark on the world. Yet, embarking on the journey of starting a business from scratch is not for the faint of heart. It demands courage, resilience, and a willingness to embrace uncertainty as you navigate uncharted waters.

In this guide, we invite you to embark on a transformative voyage—one that will take you from the genesis of an idea to the triumphant launch of your business into the vast expanse of the marketplace. Each stage of this odyssey presents its own set of challenges and opportunities, requiring careful navigation and steadfast determination.

At the outset lies the spark of inspiration—the moment when a seed of an idea takes root in the fertile soil of your imagination. It may emerge from a personal passion, a keen observation of unmet needs, or a desire to innovate and disrupt the status quo. Whatever its origin, nurturing this seed into a viable business concept requires creativity, vision, and a willingness to challenge conventional thinking.

As you embark on the journey of idea generation, you'll find yourself exploring new horizons, charting unexplored territories, and daring to dream of what could be. But dreams alone are not enough; they must be grounded in reality through rigorous market research and analysis. This is where you'll delve into the depths of your target market, uncovering insights into consumer preferences, competitive landscapes, and industry trends.

Armed with this knowledge, you'll set sail on the next leg of your journey: crafting a business plan that serves as a compass, guiding your strategic decisions and charting a course toward your goals. Your business plan is more than a mere document; it's a blueprint for success—a roadmap that outlines your mission, vision, and strategies for achieving sustainable growth and profitability.

But even the most meticulously crafted plans are subject to the whims of fate and the uncertainties of the market. Thus, securing funding becomes a critical milestone on your entrepreneurial voyage. Whether through bootstrapping, seeking investors, or crowdfunding, obtaining the necessary capital to fuel your venture requires resourcefulness, resilience, and a compelling pitch that captures the imagination of potential backers.

With funding secured and your course plotted, you'll turn your attention to the legal and logistical considerations of establishing your business. Choosing the right legal structure, navigating regulatory requirements, and securing the appropriate licenses and permits are essential steps in laying a solid foundation for your enterprise.

As you prepare to set sail into the marketplace, you'll need to equip yourself with the tools and resources necessary to navigate the turbulent waters of entrepreneurship. This includes building a strong brand identity, developing a comprehensive marketing and sales strategy, and establishing robust operational systems and processes.

But perhaps the most vital compass on your journey is your unwavering commitment to customer service and satisfaction. In the crowded sea of commerce, it's the personal touch, the attention to detail, and the willingness to go above and beyond that sets successful businesses apart from the rest.

Along the way, you'll encounter storms and challenges—moments of doubt, setbacks, and unexpected obstacles that test your resolve. But like seasoned sailors, you'll learn to adapt, innovate, and navigate through the roughest seas, emerging stronger and more resilient with each passing tempest.

As you near the shores of success, you'll look back on the journey with pride and gratitude—for the lessons learned, the challenges overcome, and the victories won. But the journey doesn't end with the launch of your business; it's merely the beginning of a new chapter—a chapter filled with opportunities for growth, expansion, and continued innovation.

So, dear voyager, as you prepare to embark on this epic journey of entrepreneurship, we offer this guide as your faithful companion— a beacon of light to guide you through the darkest nights and the roughest seas. With courage in your heart, vision in your mind, and determination in your spirit, set sail and let your entrepreneurial dreams carry you to new horizons. Fair winds and following seas await—bon voyage!

[A]

Nurturing Ideas into Innovation: A Comprehensive Exploration of Idea Generation Strategies for Aspiring Entrepreneurs"

In the vast landscape of entrepreneurship, the journey often begins with a single spark—an idea that ignites the imagination and sets the wheels of innovation in motion. Idea generation is the foundational step in starting a business from scratch, and it's a process that requires both creativity and strategic thinking. In this section, we will embark on a comprehensive exploration of idea generation strategies tailored specifically for aspiring entrepreneurs.

Explore Your Passions and Interests:
The first step in idea generation is to reflect on your passions, interests, and areas of expertise. What topics or activities excite you? What problems or challenges do you find yourself drawn to? By tapping into your passions, you can uncover potential business ideas that align with your personal values and strengths.

Identify Unmet Needs and Pain Points:
Pay close attention to the world around you and observe the challenges that people face in their daily lives. What problems do they encounter? What frustrations do they experience? By identifying unmet needs and pain points, you can identify opportunities for innovation and develop solutions that address real-world problems.

Brainstorm Ideas Freely:
Set aside time for brainstorming sessions where you can generate ideas freely without judgment. Use techniques such as mind mapping, brainstorming exercises, or idea boards to stimulate creativity and explore different possibilities. Encourage collaboration by involving others in the brainstorming process, whether it's friends, family members, or colleagues.

Research Market Trends and Opportunities:
Stay informed about market trends, emerging technologies, and industry developments relevant to your areas of interest. Conduct market research to identify gaps in the market or underserved niches where you can carve out a unique position. Look for opportunities to leverage your expertise or interests in a way that meets the needs of a specific target audience.

Seek Inspiration from Diverse Sources:
Draw inspiration from a wide range of sources, including books, articles, podcasts, TED talks, and industry events. Expose yourself to different perspectives, disciplines, and industries to spark new ideas and insights. Look for patterns, analogies, or connections between seemingly unrelated concepts that could inspire innovative solutions.

Prototype and Experiment:
Once you have generated potential business ideas, create prototypes or minimum viable products (MVPs) to test your concepts and gather feedback from potential customers. Use tools such as mockups, prototypes, or landing pages to visualize your ideas and communicate them effectively. Iterate on your prototypes based on user feedback and insights gathered from testing.

Evaluate Feasibility and Viability:

Assess the feasibility and viability of each idea by considering factors such as market demand, competition, scalability, and resource requirements. Conduct a SWOT analysis (Strengths, Weaknesses, Opportunities, Threats) to evaluate the strengths and weaknesses of each idea and identify potential risks and challenges. Choose ideas that align with your goals, resources, and capabilities.

Refine and Narrow Down Your Ideas:

Refine your list of ideas based on feedback, research, and evaluation criteria. Narrow down your focus to the most promising ideas that have the greatest potential for success. Consider factors such as your passion for the idea, market demand, competitive landscape, and differentiation strategy when making your final selection.

Validate Your Ideas with Real-World Feedback:

Before committing to a business idea, validate it with real-world feedback from potential customers or stakeholders. Conduct surveys, interviews, or focus groups to gather insights into customer preferences, pain points, and willingness to pay for your solution. Use this feedback to refine your idea further and ensure that it resonates with your target market.

Stay Curious and Open-Minded:

Idea generation is an ongoing process that requires curiosity, open-mindedness, and a willingness to explore new possibilities. Stay curious about the world around you, and remain open to serendipitous discoveries and unexpected opportunities. Keep challenging yourself to think creatively and push the boundaries of conventional thinking.

In conclusion, idea generation is the cornerstone of entrepreneurship—a process of discovery, innovation, and imagination that lays the foundation for building successful businesses. By leveraging your passions, observing the world around you, collaborating with others, and staying open to new ideas, you can unlock a wealth of entrepreneurial opportunities and embark on a journey of transformation and growth.

[B]

Navigating the Market Landscape: A Comprehensive Guide to Effective Market Research for Aspiring Entrepreneurs

Market research is a crucial aspect of starting a business from scratch. It involves gathering and analyzing information about your target market, competitors, industry trends, and customer preferences to make informed decisions and validate your business idea. In this section, we will delve into the intricacies of market research and explore effective strategies for aspiring entrepreneurs.

Define Your Target Market:
The first step in market research is to define your target market—the group of people or businesses that are most likely to purchase your product or service. Consider factors such as demographics (age, gender, income), psychographics (lifestyle, values, interests), and behavior (buying habits, preferences). Develop detailed buyer personas to better understand the needs, preferences, and pain points of your target audience.

Conduct Secondary Research:
Start by gathering information from existing sources such as industry reports, market studies, government publications, and online databases. Look for data on market size, growth trends, competitive landscape, and consumer behavior. Analyze competitor websites, social media profiles, and customer reviews to gain insights into their strengths, weaknesses, and market positioning.

Explore Primary Research Methods:
Supplement secondary research with primary research methods to gather firsthand insights from your target market. This may include conducting surveys, interviews, focus groups,

or observational studies to gather qualitative and quantitative data. Use online survey tools, social media platforms, or email marketing campaigns to reach your target audience and solicit feedback on your business idea.

Design Effective Surveys and Questionnaires:
When designing surveys and questionnaires, ensure that they are clear, concise, and unbiased. Use a mix of closed-ended and open-ended questions to gather both quantitative and qualitative data. Consider factors such as survey length, question wording, and response options to maximize response rates and accuracy.

Conduct In-Depth Interviews:
In-depth interviews provide an opportunity to delve deeper into the thoughts, feelings, and motivations of your target audience. Conduct one-on-one interviews with potential customers or industry experts to gain valuable insights into their needs, pain points, and decision-making process. Listen actively, ask probing questions, and encourage participants to share their honest opinions and experiences.

Facilitate Focus Groups:
Focus groups bring together a diverse group of individuals to discuss a specific topic or product concept in a structured setting. Use focus groups to gather feedback on your business idea, prototype, or marketing messaging. Choose participants that represent your target market and facilitate discussions to uncover insights, preferences, and concerns.

Analyze and Interpret Data:
Once you have collected data from your market research efforts, it's time to analyze and interpret the findings. Look for patterns, trends, and correlations in the data to identify key insights and actionable takeaways. Use data visualization tools such as charts, graphs, and heatmaps to present your findings in a clear and compelling manner.

Assess Market Demand and Competition:
Evaluate the demand for your product or service by assessing factors such as market size, growth potential, and competitive intensity. Identify direct and indirect competitors, analyze their strengths and weaknesses, and assess their market positioning and pricing strategies. Use this information to identify gaps in the market and opportunities for differentiation.

Validate Your Business Idea:
Use the insights gathered from market research to validate your business idea and refine your value proposition. Assess whether there is a sufficient market demand for your product or service, and whether you have a competitive advantage that sets you apart from rivals. Adjust your business concept, target market, or positioning as needed based on market feedback and analysis.

Iterate and Refine:
Market research is an ongoing process that should inform every stage of your business journey. Continuously gather feedback from customers, monitor market trends, and stay attuned to changes in consumer behavior and preferences. Use this information to iterate and refine your business strategy, product offerings, and marketing tactics to stay ahead of the curve and remain competitive in the market.

In conclusion, effective market research is essential for guiding strategic decision-making, minimizing risks, and maximizing opportunities for success in entrepreneurship. By understanding your target market, assessing market demand and competition, and validating your business idea with real-world data, you can lay a solid foundation for building a thriving business from scratch. Embrace market research as a powerful tool for driving innovation, differentiation, and sustainable growth, and let it guide you on your entrepreneurial journey towards success.

[C]

Charting Your Course: A Comprehensive Guide to Crafting a Business Plan for Aspiring Entrepreneurs

A business plan serves as a roadmap for your entrepreneurial journey—a strategic document that outlines your vision, goals, and strategies for building a successful business from scratch. In this section, we will explore the essential elements of a business plan and provide practical guidance for aspiring entrepreneurs on how to craft a comprehensive and compelling document.

Executive Summary:
- The executive summary is the gateway to your business plan, offering a condensed overview of your entire document.
- It should include key elements such as your business concept, target market, competitive advantage, revenue projections, and funding requirements.
- Despite its placement at the beginning of the plan, it's often written last to ensure it captures the essence of your business plan effectively.
- Aim for clarity and brevity, keeping it concise while still providing enough information to entice the reader to delve deeper into your plan.

Company Overview:
- Provide a detailed description of your business, outlining its mission, vision, values, and objectives.
- Describe the products or services you offer, emphasizing their unique features and benefits.
- Discuss your target market, including demographics, psychographics, and any niche segments you plan to target.

- Explain your business's legal structure (e.g., sole proprietorship, partnership, LLC, corporation) and ownership details.

Market Analysis:

- Conduct a thorough analysis of your target market, industry trends, and competitive landscape.
- Identify and profile your target market segments, detailing their needs, preferences, and purchasing behavior.
- Evaluate market size, growth potential, and key drivers shaping the industry.
- Analyze competitors' strengths, weaknesses, market positioning, pricing strategies, and customer acquisition tactics.

Marketing Strategy:

- Outline your marketing strategy for reaching and engaging your target audience effectively.
- Define your product positioning, highlighting its unique value proposition and differentiation from competitors.
- Describe your pricing strategy, distribution channels, and promotional tactics (e.g., advertising, PR, digital marketing).
- Detail your brand identity, messaging strategy, and plans for building brand awareness and loyalty.

Operations Plan:

- Detail the operational aspects of your business, including production processes, supply chain management, and inventory control.
- Describe your facilities, equipment, and technology requirements, as well as any strategic partnerships or outsourcing arrangements.
- Outline your staffing plan, organizational structure, and key roles and responsibilities within the company.

- Discuss any regulatory or compliance considerations relevant to your operations.

Financial Projections:
- Prepare detailed financial projections for your business, including income statements, cash flow forecasts, and balance sheets.
- Estimate your startup costs, operating expenses, and revenue projections for the first three to five years of operation.
- Use realistic assumptions and conservative estimates to ensure accuracy and credibility.
- Include key financial metrics such as gross margin, net profit, break-even analysis, and return on investment (ROI).

Funding Request:
- If seeking funding, outline your funding requirements and how you plan to use the funds effectively.
- Specify the amount of funding needed, the sources of funding you're pursuing (e.g., loans, investors, crowdfunding), and the terms and conditions you're offering in return.
- Provide a compelling justification for why your business is a worthy investment opportunity, highlighting its growth potential, market traction, and competitive advantage.

Appendices:
- Include any supporting documents or supplementary information that are relevant to your business plan.
- This may include market research reports, industry analysis, resumes of key team members, legal documents, or letters of intent from potential customers or partners.
- Organize the appendices logically and provide clear references to relevant sections within the main body of the business plan.

Crafting a business plan requires careful research, analysis, and strategic thinking. Here are some tips to help you create a comprehensive and compelling document:

- **Start with an outline:** Begin by outlining the key sections and sub-sections of your business plan to organize your thoughts and ideas effectively.
- **Tailor your plan to your audience:** Consider who will be reading your business plan and tailor the content and tone accordingly. Investors may be more interested in financial projections and ROI potential, while lenders may focus on risk mitigation and repayment strategies.
- **Be concise and to the point:** Keep your writing clear, concise, and focused on the most important information. Avoid jargon or technical language that may be confusing to readers.
- **Use visuals and graphics:** Incorporate charts, graphs, and tables to illustrate key data and trends visually. Visual elements can help break up text and make complex information easier to understand.
- **Seek feedback and revisions:** Once you've drafted your business plan, seek feedback from mentors, advisors, or peers to identify areas for improvement. Revise and refine your plan based on their input to ensure clarity, coherence, and completeness.

Once you have compiled detailed explanations for each subheading, arrange them in a logical sequence to create a comprehensive business plan. Be sure to review and revise the plan thoroughly to ensure clarity, coherence, and completeness before sharing it with stakeholders, investors, or potential partners.

In conclusion, a well-crafted business plan is an indispensable tool for aspiring entrepreneurs, providing a roadmap for success and a blueprint for turning your vision into reality. By following the guidelines outlined in this section and dedicating time and effort to thorough research and strategic planning, you can create a compelling business plan that inspires confidence in investors, lenders, and stakeholders, and sets you on the path to entrepreneurial success.

[D]
Securing Funding: A Comprehensive Guide for Entrepreneurs Seeking Capital for Their Startups

Securing funding is a critical milestone in the journey of starting a business. Whether you're launching a tech startup, opening a small retail shop, or pursuing a new creative venture, having access to capital is essential for turning your entrepreneurial vision into reality. In this comprehensive guide, we will explore the various avenues for securing funding and provide practical strategies for entrepreneurs seeking capital for their startups.

Assess Funding Needs:

Before embarking on your quest for funding, it's essential to assess your startup's financial needs thoroughly. Calculate the capital required to cover startup costs, operating expenses, inventory purchases, marketing initiatives, and any other financial obligations. Be realistic and conservative in your estimates to ensure you have adequate funding to support your business through the initial stages.

Determine Funding Sources:

There are numerous sources of funding available to entrepreneurs, each with its own advantages, requirements, and considerations. Consider the following funding sources and determine which ones align best with your business goals and financial needs:

- **Personal Savings:** Many entrepreneurs use personal savings as the initial source of funding for their startups. While this option allows you to maintain full control over your business and avoid debt, it may limit the amount of capital available for growth and expansion.

- **Friends and Family:** Friends and family members can be a valuable source of early-stage funding for your startup. When seeking funding from loved ones, be transparent about the risks involved and formalize the arrangement with clear terms and agreements to avoid potential conflicts down the road.
- **Angel Investors:** Angel investors are affluent individuals who provide capital to startups in exchange for equity ownership. Angel investors often have entrepreneurial experience and can provide valuable mentorship, connections, and strategic guidance in addition to funding.
- **Venture Capital:** Venture capital (VC) firms invest larger amounts of capital in high-growth startups in exchange for equity ownership. VC funding is typically reserved for startups with scalable business models, strong growth potential, and a clear path to profitability.
- **Bank Loans:** Banks and financial institutions offer various types of loans, including term loans, lines of credit, and Small Business Administration (SBA) loans, to provide funding for startups. Bank loans require collateral and a strong credit history, and they often involve repayment with interest over a specified period.
- **Crowdfunding:** Crowdfunding platforms allow entrepreneurs to raise capital from a large number of individual investors, often in exchange for rewards, equity, or debt. Crowdfunding can be an effective way to validate your business idea, build a customer base, and raise capital without giving up equity or taking on debt.
- **Government Grants and Programs:** Government agencies offer grants, loans, and other financial assistance programs to support startups, especially those in certain industries or geographic regions. Research government programs and

eligibility requirements, and apply for grants or loans that align with your business's objectives and criteria.

- **Prepare a Funding Pitch:**
  Once you've identified potential funding sources, it's essential to prepare a compelling funding pitch that effectively communicates your business idea, market opportunity, competitive advantage, financial projections, and funding requirements. Tailor your pitch to each potential investor or funding source, highlighting the aspects that are most relevant and compelling to them.

- **Due Diligence:**
  Investors will conduct due diligence to evaluate the potential risks and returns of investing in your startup. Be prepared to provide detailed financial statements, business plans, market research, legal documents, and other relevant information to support your funding request. Transparency and honesty are crucial during this process, as investors will be looking for evidence of your startup's viability and growth potential.

- **Negotiate Terms:**
  If you receive funding offers from investors or lenders, it's essential to negotiate terms that align with your business goals and objectives. Consider factors such as equity ownership, valuation, board representation, voting rights, and exit strategies when negotiating funding terms. Seek guidance from legal and financial advisors to ensure that all agreements are fair, legally sound, and protect your interests.

- **Legal and Financial Documentation:**
  Once funding agreements are reached, formalize the arrangements with legal and financial documentation, including term sheets, investment contracts, shareholder agreements, promissory notes, and loan agreements. Work closely with legal and financial professionals to ensure that all

documents are properly drafted, reviewed, and executed, and that they comply with applicable laws and regulations.

- **Use Funding Wisely:**
  Once you secure funding for your startup, it's crucial to use it wisely to achieve your business objectives and milestones. Develop a detailed budget and financial plan to allocate funds strategically, ensuring that resources are utilized efficiently and effectively. Regularly monitor your startup's financial performance and make adjustments as needed to stay on track and maximize the impact of your funding.

Securing funding is a pivotal step in the entrepreneurial journey, enabling startups to fund their operations, pursue growth opportunities, and ultimately achieve success. By assessing funding needs, identifying suitable funding sources, preparing a compelling pitch, conducting due diligence, negotiating terms, formalizing agreements, and using funds wisely, entrepreneurs can increase their chances of securing the capital needed to bring their startup visions to life.

[E]

Choosing the Right Legal Structure: A Comprehensive Guide for Entrepreneurs

A legal structure refers to the formal framework or organization through which a business operates and conducts its activities. It defines the legal status, ownership, governance, and operational parameters of a business entity. Choosing the right legal structure is a critical decision for any entrepreneur, as it impacts various aspects of your business, including liability, taxes, management, and compliance requirements. In this comprehensive guide, we will explore the different legal structures available to entrepreneurs and provide practical guidance for selecting the one that best suits your business needs and goals.

The following are the different types of Legal Structure and their functions:

➢ **Sole Proprietorship:**
- A sole proprietorship is the simplest and most common form of business structure, in which the business is owned and operated by a single individual.
- In a sole proprietorship, the owner has complete control over the business and its operations, but they are also personally liable for any debts, obligations, or legal liabilities incurred by the business.
- Sole proprietors report business income and expenses on their personal tax returns and are subject to self-employment taxes.

➢ **Partnership:**
- A partnership is a business structure in which two or more individuals share ownership and management responsibilities.
- There are two main types of partnerships: General Partnerships, in which all partners share equally in the profits, losses, and liabilities of the business, and Limited Partnerships, in which one or more partners have limited liability and are not involved in the day-to-day operations of the business.
- Partnerships are governed by a partnership agreement, which outlines the rights, responsibilities, and obligations of each partner.

➢ **Limited Liability Company (LLC):**
- A limited liability company (LLC) is a hybrid business structure that combines the limited liability protection of a corporation with the flexibility and tax advantages of a partnership or sole proprietorship.
- LLC owners, known as members, are not personally liable for the debts, obligations, or legal liabilities of the business, and their personal assets are protected from business creditors.
- LLCs offer flexibility in management structure and taxation, allowing members to choose how the business is managed and taxed (e.g., as a partnership, corporation, or disregarded entity).
- LLCs are relatively easy to form and maintain, with fewer regulatory requirements and formalities compared to corporations.

- ➢ **Corporation:**
  - A corporation is a separate legal entity that is owned by shareholders and managed by a board of directors.
  - Corporations offer limited liability protection to shareholders, meaning their personal assets are generally shielded from the debts and liabilities of the business.
  - Corporations have a more formal structure and governance requirements than other business structures, including the adoption of bylaws, holding regular shareholder and board meetings, and maintaining corporate records.
  - There are two main types of corporations: C corporations, which are subject to double taxation (at both the corporate and shareholder levels), and S corporations, which are pass-through entities that avoid double taxation by electing to be taxed under Subchapter S of the Internal Revenue Code.

- ➢ **Nonprofit Organization:**
  - A nonprofit organization is a type of corporation that is organized for charitable, religious, educational, or other public service purposes.
  - Nonprofits are exempt from federal income tax and may be eligible for state tax exemptions, as well as grants, donations, and other sources of funding.
  - Nonprofits are governed by a board of directors and must comply with specific regulations and reporting requirements to maintain their tax-exempt status.

When choosing a legal structure for your business, consider the following factors:

- ✓ **Liability Protection:** Assess the level of liability protection offered by each legal structure and choose one that best protects your personal assets from business debts and liabilities.

✓ **Tax Implications:** Evaluate the tax implications of each legal structure, including income taxes, self-employment taxes, and compliance requirements, and choose the one that offers the most favorable tax treatment for your business.

✓ **Management and Control:** Consider how you want your business to be managed and controlled, including the level of autonomy, decision-making authority, and governance structure, and choose a legal structure that aligns with your preferences.

✓ **Flexibility and Formalities:** Compare the flexibility and regulatory requirements of each legal structure, including formation and maintenance costs, ongoing compliance obligations, and administrative burdens, and choose one that strikes the right balance for your business needs.

✓ **Future Growth and Expansion:** Consider the long-term goals and growth plans for your business, including the potential for raising capital, attracting investors, and expanding into new markets, and choose a legal structure that supports your growth objectives.

✓ **Professional Advice:** Consult with legal and financial advisors to understand the legal and tax implications of each legal structure and make an informed decision based on your specific circumstances, industry, and business objectives.

By carefully considering these factors and weighing the pros and cons of each legal structure, entrepreneurs can choose the right one to protect their assets, minimize taxes, and set their businesses up for success.

[F]
Navigating Financing Options: A Comprehensive Guide for Entrepreneurs

Embarking on the journey of starting a business is an exhilarating endeavor, filled with opportunities for growth, innovation, and success. However, one of the most critical aspects of turning your entrepreneurial vision into reality is securing the necessary funding to fuel your venture's growth and development.

In this comprehensive guide, we will explore the intricacies of securing funding and navigating the diverse landscape of financing options available to entrepreneurs. From assessing your funding needs to finalizing legal documentation, we'll cover every step of the funding journey, providing you with the insights and strategies needed to make informed decisions about funding your business.

But beyond merely securing funding, it's essential for entrepreneurs to understand the role that financing plays in their journey. Financing isn't just about obtaining capital; it's about strategically leveraging resources to drive growth, achieve milestones, and position your business for long-term success.

By including both "Securing Funding" and "Financing" in our guide, we aim to provide you with a comprehensive understanding of the funding process. From identifying sources of capital to negotiating terms and selecting the right financing option for your business, we'll equip you with the knowledge and tools needed to navigate the complex world of business financing with confidence.

Whether you're launching a tech startup, opening a small retail shop, or pursuing a new creative venture, securing funding and understanding financing options are essential components of your entrepreneurial journey. So, let's dive in and explore how you can fund your dreams and turn your business ideas into reality.

- ✓ **Bootstrapping:**
  - Bootstrapping involves funding your business with personal savings, revenue generated from early sales, or other non-traditional sources of capital.
  - Bootstrapping allows you to retain full control over your business and avoid taking on debt or diluting ownership, but it may limit your ability to scale quickly.

- ✓ **Friends and Family:**
  - Friends and family members can be a valuable source of early-stage funding for your business.
  - When seeking funding from loved ones, be transparent about the risks involved and formalize the arrangement with clear terms and agreements to avoid potential conflicts.
- ✓ **Angel Investors:**
  - Angel investors are affluent individuals who provide capital to startups in exchange for equity ownership.
  - Angel investors often have entrepreneurial experience and can provide valuable mentorship, connections, and strategic guidance in addition to funding.
- ✓ **Venture Capital:**
  - Venture capital (VC) firms invest larger amounts of capital in high-growth startups in exchange for equity ownership.
  - VC funding is typically reserved for startups with scalable business models, strong growth potential, and a clear path to profitability.
- ✓ **Bank Loans:**
  - Banks and financial institutions offer various types of loans, including term loans, lines of credit, and Small Business Administration (SBA) loans, to provide funding for startups.

- Bank loans require collateral and a strong credit history, and they often involve repayment with interest over a specified period.

✓ **Crowdfunding:**

- Crowdfunding platforms allow entrepreneurs to raise capital from a large number of individual investors, often in exchange for rewards, equity, or debt.
- Crowdfunding can be an effective way to validate your business idea, build a customer base, and raise capital without giving up equity or taking on debt.

✓ **Government Grants and Programs:**

- Government agencies offer grants, loans, and other financial assistance programs to support startups, especially those in certain industries or geographic regions.
- Research government programs and eligibility requirements, and apply for grants or loans that align with your business's objectives and criteria.

✓ **Accelerators and Incubators:**

- Accelerators and incubators are programs that provide startups with funding, mentorship, resources, and networking opportunities in exchange for equity.
- Participating in an accelerator or incubator program can help startups accelerate their growth, validate their business model, and attract additional funding from investors.

✓ **Corporate Partnerships and Strategic Investors:**

- Partnering with established corporations or securing investments from strategic investors can provide startups with not only capital but also access to resources, distribution channels, and industry expertise.
- Strategic partnerships and investments can help startups scale more quickly and mitigate risks associated with market entry and expansion.

✓ **Alternative Financing Options:**
  - In addition to traditional sources of funding, entrepreneurs can explore alternative financing options such as revenue-based financing, equipment leasing, factoring, and peer-to-peer lending.
  - Alternative financing options may offer more flexibility, lower costs, or faster access to capital compared to traditional funding sources.

When evaluating financing options for your business, consider factors such as the amount of funding needed, the stage of your business, your growth plans, and the terms and conditions offered by each funding source. It's essential to conduct thorough research, seek advice from financial professionals, and carefully evaluate the potential risks and rewards of each financing option before making a decision. By exploring a diverse range of financing options and tailoring your approach to your specific business needs, you can increase your chances of securing the funding needed to fuel your entrepreneurial journey and achieve success.

[G]
Choosing the Right Location and Infrastructure: Factors to Consider for Your Business.

Selecting the right location and infrastructure for your business is crucial for its success. The location influences various aspects of your operations, including accessibility, visibility, customer demographics, competition, and operating costs. In this detailed guide, we will explore the factors to consider when choosing a location and infrastructure for your business and provide practical tips to help you make informed decisions.

Market Analysis:

- Conduct a thorough market analysis to understand your target audience, competition, and market trends.
- Identify the demographics, preferences, and behaviors of your target customers to determine the most suitable location for your business.
- Evaluate the demand for your products or services in different areas and assess the level of competition you'll face in each location.

Accessibility and Visibility:

- Choose a location that is easily accessible to your target customers, suppliers, and employees.
- Consider factors such as proximity to major roads, public transportation options, parking availability, and foot traffic.
- Prioritize visibility to attract passing customers and increase brand exposure. Select a location with high visibility from main roads or in busy commercial areas.

Foot Traffic and Surrounding Businesses:

- Assess the level of foot traffic in potential locations to gauge the potential for attracting customers.
- Consider the types of businesses and establishments in the vicinity and their relevance to your target market.
- Determine if clustering with complementary businesses can benefit your business by increasing customer traffic and cross-promotional opportunities.

Operating Costs:

- Evaluate the operating costs associated with different locations, including rent or lease prices, utilities, taxes, and insurance.
- Compare the cost of doing business in various areas and consider the impact on your budget and profitability.
- Look for opportunities to negotiate favorable lease terms or incentives with landlords to reduce overhead expenses.

Infrastructure and Facilities:

- Assess the infrastructure and facilities available in potential locations to ensure they meet your business needs.
- Consider factors such as the size and layout of the space, amenities, utilities, internet connectivity, and security features.
- Evaluate the condition of the building and any necessary renovations or improvements required to accommodate your business operations.

Zoning and Regulations:

- Familiarize yourself with local zoning regulations, building codes, and permit requirements that may impact your choice of location.
- Ensure that the chosen location is zoned for your type of business and compliant with all regulatory requirements.

- Obtain necessary permits and licenses before establishing your business to avoid potential legal issues or fines.

Future Growth and Expansion:

- Consider the scalability and long-term potential of the location for accommodating future growth and expansion.
- Assess whether the chosen location can support your business's evolving needs and accommodate increases in customer demand, staff, or inventory.
- Plan for future expansion by negotiating flexible lease terms or exploring options for adjacent spaces or satellite locations.

Brand Image and Customer Perception:

- Choose a location that aligns with your brand image and communicates the right message to your target customers.
- Consider how the location reflects the values, aesthetics, and positioning of your brand.
- Select a location that enhances your brand's reputation and fosters positive customer perceptions.

Local Community and Culture:

- Evaluate the local community and culture of potential locations to ensure alignment with your business values and objectives.
- Consider factors such as community demographics, lifestyle preferences, and cultural norms that may impact your business's success.
- Engage with local stakeholders, business associations, and community leaders to gain insights into the area's dynamics and opportunities.

Risk Assessment and Contingency Planning:

- Identify potential risks and challenges associated with each location and develop contingency plans to mitigate them.

- Consider factors such as natural disasters, economic downturns, and changes in consumer behavior that may affect the viability of the location.
- Maintain flexibility and adaptability in your location strategy to respond to changing market conditions and unforeseen challenges.

By carefully considering these factors and conducting thorough due diligence, you can select the right location and infrastructure for your business that aligns with your goals, enhances your brand, and maximizes your chances of success. Remember that choosing a location is not just about finding a physical space; it's about positioning your business strategically to thrive in its market environment.

[H]
Building Your Brand: Strategies for Effective Brand Development

Brand development is the strategic process of creating and enhancing a brand's identity, personality, and reputation to establish a distinct and memorable presence in the minds of consumers. It involves defining the brand's mission, values, and positioning in the market, understanding the target audience, crafting compelling brand messaging, designing visual elements such as logos and brand assets, and creating consistent brand experiences across all touchpoints.

Brand development aims to differentiate a business from its competitors, build emotional connections with customers, foster brand loyalty, and drive long-term success. It requires careful planning, research, and creative execution to create a brand identity that resonates with the target audience and effectively communicates the brand's unique value proposition.

The process of brand development may include activities such as market research, customer analysis, brand strategy formulation, logo and visual identity design, brand messaging development, brand storytelling, brand guidelines creation, and ongoing brand management and monitoring. By investing in brand development, businesses can create a strong and enduring brand that leaves a lasting impression on consumers and contributes to business growth and success. Brand development is a fundamental aspect of starting and growing a business. A strong brand not only differentiates your business from competitors but also creates emotional connections with customers, fosters loyalty, and drives long-term success. In this detailed guide, we will explore the strategies and steps involved in building a compelling brand that resonates with your target audience and sets your business apart.

Define Your Brand Identity:

- Start by defining your brand identity, which encompasses your brand's mission, values, personality, and positioning in the market.
- Consider what sets your business apart from competitors and how you want to be perceived by customers.
- Develop a brand identity statement that succinctly communicates who you are, what you stand for, and why you matter to your target audience.

Understand Your Target Audience:

- Gain a deep understanding of your target audience, including their demographics, preferences, needs, and pain points.
- Conduct market research, surveys, and customer interviews to gather insights into your audience's motivations, behaviors, and buying habits.
- Use this information to create detailed customer personas that represent your ideal customers and guide your brand messaging and marketing efforts.

Craft Your Brand Messaging:

- Develop clear and compelling brand messaging that communicates your unique value proposition and resonates with your target audience.
- Define key messages that highlight the benefits of your products or services, address customer pain points, and evoke emotion.
- Ensure consistency in your brand messaging across all touchpoints, including your website, social media channels, marketing materials, and customer interactions.

Create a Memorable Brand Name and Logo:

- Choose a memorable and distinctive brand name that reflects your brand identity and is easy to pronounce, spell, and remember.

- Design a visually appealing and versatile logo that represents your brand's personality and communicates its essence effectively. - Consider working with a professional graphic designer or branding agency to create a logo that captures the essence of your brand and resonates with your target audience.

Develop Brand Visuals and Assets:

- Create a cohesive visual identity for your brand, including colors, fonts, imagery, and design elements.
- Ensure consistency in your brand visuals across all marketing materials and touchpoints to reinforce brand recognition and recall.
- Design branded assets such as business cards, letterheads, packaging, and signage that reflect your brand's personality and values.

Build a Strong Online Presence:

- Establish a professional and user-friendly website that showcases your brand story, products or services, and value proposition.
- Optimize your website for search engines (SEO) to improve visibility and attract organic traffic from potential customers.
- Leverage social media platforms to engage with your audience, share valuable content, and build relationships with customers and followers.

Deliver Consistent Brand Experience:

- Ensure consistency in the delivery of your brand experience across all customer touchpoints, from the first interaction to post-purchase support.
- Train your staff to embody your brand values and deliver exceptional customer service that aligns with your brand promise.

- Monitor customer feedback and satisfaction to identify areas for improvement and refine your brand experience over time.

Cultivate Brand Advocates and Ambassadors:
- Encourage satisfied customers to become brand advocates by sharing their positive experiences with others and recommending your products or services.
- Identify influencers, industry experts, and loyal customers who align with your brand values and engage them as brand ambassadors to amplify your reach and credibility.
- Foster a sense of community and belonging among your customers to cultivate brand loyalty and advocacy.

Evolve and Adapt Your Brand:
- Stay attuned to market trends, customer feedback, and competitive landscape to evolve and adapt your brand over time.
- Continuously refine your brand messaging, visuals, and experiences to remain relevant and resonate with changing consumer preferences.
- Embrace innovation and experimentation to differentiate your brand and stay ahead of the competition in a dynamic marketplace.

By following these strategies and investing in brand development, you can create a strong and distinctive brand that captivates your target audience, fosters loyalty, and drives business growth. Remember that building a brand is not a one-time effort but an ongoing journey that requires dedication, creativity, and authenticity.

[I]
Launching Your Business: Marketing and Sales Strategies for Startups

Starting a business from scratch requires careful planning and execution, especially when it comes to marketing and sales. In this section, we'll explore practical strategies to kickstart your business and effectively promote your products or services to attract customers and generate revenue.

1. Know Your Audience from Day One:
- Understand your target audience's demographics, preferences, and needs before launching your business.
- Conduct market research and create customer personas to guide your marketing and sales efforts.

2. Craft a Compelling Value Proposition:
- Define a clear and compelling value proposition that communicates the unique benefits of your offerings to potential customers.
- Highlight how your products or services solve a problem or fulfill a need better than competitors.

3. Start with a Lean Marketing Approach:
- Begin with cost-effective marketing tactics such as social media marketing, content creation, and email campaigns.
- Focus on channels that offer the most bang for your buck and align with your target audience's behavior.

4. Build Your Brand Presence:
- Establish a professional online presence through a website and social media profiles.
- Create consistent branding elements such as logos, colors, and messaging to reinforce your brand identity.

5. **Leverage Your Network:**
- Tap into your personal and professional networks to spread the word about your business.
- Encourage referrals and word-of-mouth marketing from friends, family, and colleagues.

6. **Focus on High-impact Marketing Activities:**
- Identify key marketing activities that have the most potential to reach your target audience and drive engagement.
- Experiment with different tactics and channels to determine what works best for your business.

7. **Start Selling Early:**
- Don't wait for perfection—start selling as soon as you have a minimum viable product or service.
- Engage with early customers to gather feedback and improve your offerings over time.

8. **Listen to Customer Feedback:**
- Actively seek feedback from customers and use it to refine your products, services, and marketing strategies.
- Address customer concerns and adapt to their needs to build trust and loyalty.

9. **Track Your Progress:**
- Implement analytics tools to track the performance of your marketing and sales efforts.
- Monitor key metrics such as website traffic, conversion rates, and customer acquisition costs to measure success.

10. **Stay Flexible and Adapt:**
- Stay agile and responsive to changes in the market, customer preferences, and competitive landscape.
- Continuously iterate on your marketing and sales strategies based on real-time data and insights.

By following these startup-focused marketing and sales strategies, you can lay a solid foundation for your business and attract your first customers while positioning yourself for long-term success. Remember that starting a business is a journey, and it's okay to adjust your approach along the way based on what works best for your unique venture.

[J]
Operation Management

Effective operations management is the cornerstone of a successful business. Whether you're launching a startup or expanding an existing venture, mastering the intricacies of operations management is essential for optimizing efficiency, controlling costs, and delivering exceptional products or services to your customers. In this section, we'll explore the fundamental principles and strategies of operations management that are crucial for building a solid foundation for your business. From process design and improvement to quality control, inventory management, and resource allocation, each aspect of operations management plays a vital role in shaping the success of your business. Let's delve deeper into these key areas and discover how you can leverage them to drive operational excellence and achieve your business goals.

Now, let's proceed to elaborate on each sub point of operations management.

Process Design: Building the Blueprint for Efficiency

Process design is the architectural blueprint of your business operations. It involves structuring and organizing workflows to optimize efficiency, minimize waste, and deliver consistent results. Here's a closer look at the key elements of process design:

1) Understanding Workflow Dynamics:

- Begin by mapping out the sequence of activities involved in your business operations. Identify each step, from the initial intake of raw materials or customer orders to the final delivery of products or services.

- Analyze the flow of work and information between different stages of the process. Look for opportunities to streamline transitions and eliminate unnecessary handoffs or delays.

2) Identifying Bottlenecks and Inefficiencies:

- Conduct a thorough analysis to identify bottlenecks—points in the process where work accumulates or slows down. Common causes of bottlenecks include resource constraints, uneven workloads, and inefficient procedures.
- Once identified, prioritize addressing bottlenecks to improve overall throughput and productivity. This might involve reallocating resources, redesigning workflows, or implementing automation solutions.

3) Streamlining Processes:

- Streamlining involves simplifying and optimizing processes to minimize complexity and maximize efficiency. Look for opportunities to standardize procedures, eliminate redundant steps, and automate repetitive tasks.
- Encourage input from frontline employees who are directly involved in executing processes. Their insights can often reveal inefficiencies or opportunities for improvement that might not be apparent from a higher-level perspective.

4) Implementing Continuous Improvement:

- Continuous improvement is an ongoing process of refinement and enhancement. Foster a culture of innovation and learning within your organization, where employees are encouraged to suggest and implement improvements.
- Establish regular review cycles to evaluate the effectiveness of process changes and identify further opportunities for optimization. Monitor key performance indicators (KPIs) to track progress and measure the impact of process improvements over time.

5) Utilizing Technology and Automation:

- Technology can play a transformative role in process design, enabling greater efficiency and scalability. Explore automation solutions, workflow management systems, and digital tools that streamline operations and reduce manual effort.
- Leverage data analytics and business intelligence tools to gain insights into process performance and identify areas for optimization. By harnessing the power of technology, you can unlock new levels of productivity and agility in your operations.

6) Ensuring Flexibility and Adaptability:

- In today's dynamic business environment, it's essential to design processes that can adapt to changing circumstances and evolving customer needs. Build flexibility into your workflows to accommodate fluctuations in demand, market conditions, and resource availability.
- Anticipate potential disruptions and develop contingency plans to mitigate their impact on operations. By proactively addressing risks and uncertainties, you can ensure continuity and resilience in your business operations.

By paying careful attention to process design, you can establish a solid foundation for your business operations and set the stage for sustainable growth and success. Invest time and resources in designing efficient and effective workflows, and you'll reap the rewards of improved productivity, enhanced quality, and greater customer satisfaction.

Supply Chain Management: Building Resilience and Efficiency
Supply chain management (SCM) is the backbone of your business's operations, encompassing the end-to-end flow of goods, services, and information from suppliers to customers. Effective supply chain management is essential for optimizing

costs, ensuring product quality, and delivering exceptional customer service. Here's a closer look at the key components of supply chain management:

1. Supplier Relationship Management:

- Cultivating strong relationships with suppliers is essential for securing reliable access to quality materials and components. Establish open lines of communication and collaborate closely with suppliers to align goals and expectations.
- Negotiate favorable terms and agreements that balance cost considerations with quality and reliability. Consider factors such as pricing, payment terms, delivery schedules, and product specifications when evaluating supplier relationships.

2. Demand Forecasting:

- Accurate demand forecasting is critical for optimizing inventory levels and production schedules. Utilize historical sales data, market trends, and customer feedback to forecast demand for your products or services.
- Invest in forecasting tools and techniques that leverage statistical models and predictive analytics to improve forecast accuracy. Regularly review and refine your demand forecasts based on changing market conditions and customer preferences.

3. Logistics Optimization:

- Logistics optimization involves optimizing transportation, warehousing, and distribution processes to minimize costs and lead times. Evaluate transportation modes, routes, and carriers to identify opportunities for efficiency improvements.
- Implement inventory optimization strategies such as cross-docking, vendor-managed inventory (VMI), and just-in-time

(JIT) delivery to reduce inventory holding costs and improve inventory turnover rates.

4. **Inventory Management:**
   - Effective inventory management is essential for balancing supply and demand while minimizing carrying costs and stockouts. Implement inventory control systems that provide real-time visibility into inventory levels and movements.
   - Utilize inventory optimization techniques such as ABC analysis, economic order quantity (EOQ), and safety stock planning to optimize inventory levels and improve inventory turnover rates.

5. **Supplier Diversity and Risk Management:**
   - Diversifying your supplier base can help mitigate risks such as supply chain disruptions, quality issues, and geopolitical uncertainties. Identify alternative suppliers and develop contingency plans to ensure business continuity.
   - Implement supply chain risk management practices such as supplier risk assessments, business continuity planning, and supply chain mapping to identify and mitigate potential risks proactively.

6. **Sustainability and Ethical Sourcing:**
   - Embracing sustainability and ethical sourcing practices can enhance your brand reputation and appeal to socially conscious consumers. Evaluate suppliers based on their environmental, social, and governance (ESG) practices and prioritize partnerships with responsible suppliers.
   - Implement supply chain sustainability initiatives such as reducing carbon emissions, minimizing waste, and promoting fair labor practices throughout your supply chain.

Technology Integration:
- Leverage technology to enhance visibility, collaboration, and efficiency across your supply chain. Implement supply chain

management software (SCMS) and enterprise resource planning (ERP) systems to centralize data and streamline processes.

- Explore emerging technologies such as blockchain, Internet of Things (IoT), and artificial intelligence (AI) to improve traceability, transparency, and predictive capabilities within your supply chain.

By focusing on these key aspects of supply chain management, you can build a resilient and efficient supply chain that supports your business's growth and success. Prioritize collaboration, transparency, and continuous improvement across all stages of the supply chain to drive value and deliver superior outcomes for your customers.

Inventory Management: Balancing Supply and Demand

Inventory management is the process of overseeing and controlling the flow of goods and materials within your business. Effective inventory management is essential for ensuring that you have the right products in the right quantities at the right time while minimizing costs and maximizing efficiency. Here's a closer look at the key components of inventory management:

❖ **Inventory Control Systems:**
  - Implement inventory control systems to track and manage inventory levels accurately. Choose a system that aligns with your business needs and provides real-time visibility into inventory movements and stock levels.
  - Utilize barcode scanning, RFID technology, or inventory management software to automate inventory tracking and streamline data collection processes.

❖ **Demand Forecasting:**
  - Forecasting demand accurately is crucial for maintaining optimal inventory levels and preventing stockouts or excess

inventory. Utilize historical sales data, market trends, and customer insights to forecast demand for your products or services.

- Consider factors such as seasonality, promotions, and market trends when developing demand forecasts. Regularly review and adjust forecasts based on changing market conditions and customer preferences.

❖ **ABC Analysis:**

- Classify inventory items based on their importance and value using ABC analysis. Category A items are high-value items that represent a significant portion of revenue, while category C items are low-value items with minimal impact on revenue.
- Allocate resources and attention accordingly, focusing on managing category A items more closely while adopting a more relaxed approach to category C items.

❖ **Inventory Turnover Optimization:**

- Inventory turnover measures how quickly inventory is sold or used within a specific period. Strive to increase inventory turnover rates by reducing excess inventory and improving demand forecasting accuracy.
- Monitor inventory turnover ratios regularly and identify opportunities to optimize inventory levels. Adjust reorder points, safety stock levels, and replenishment strategies to align with demand fluctuations and market trends.

❖ **Safety Stock Management:**

- Safety stock is additional inventory held as a buffer against variability in demand or supply. Determine appropriate safety stock levels based on factors such as lead times, demand variability, and supplier reliability.
- Implement robust safety stock management practices to ensure adequate inventory availability while minimizing excess inventory holding costs. Regularly review and adjust

safety stock levels based on changing business conditions and performance metrics.

❖ **Supplier Collaboration and Vendor Management:**
- Collaborate closely with suppliers to optimize inventory management across the supply chain. Implement vendor-managed inventory (VMI) or consignment inventory programs to improve inventory visibility and control.
- Establish clear communication channels and performance metrics to monitor supplier performance and address any issues or discrepancies promptly. Build strong relationships with suppliers based on trust, transparency, and mutual benefit.

❖ **Just-in-Time (JIT) Inventory Management:**
- JIT inventory management aims to minimize inventory holding costs by synchronizing production and inventory levels with customer demand. Produce or procure goods just in time to meet customer orders, reducing the need for excess inventory.
- Implement JIT principles such as lean manufacturing, pull-based production, and kanban systems to streamline workflows and reduce waste throughout the supply chain.

By implementing effective inventory management practices, you can optimize inventory levels, reduce costs, and improve overall operational efficiency. Prioritize accuracy, visibility, and collaboration across all aspects of inventory management to meet customer demand effectively and drive business success.

Quality Control: Ensuring Excellence in Products and Services
Quality control is the process of maintaining consistent quality standards in your products or services to meet customer expectations and regulatory requirements. It involves monitoring, evaluating, and improving processes to ensure that defects and

errors are minimized, and customer satisfaction is maximized. Here's a closer look at the key components of quality control:

➢ **Establishing Quality Standards:**
Define clear quality standards and specifications for your products or services based on customer requirements, industry standards, and regulatory guidelines. These standards serve as benchmarks for measuring performance and ensuring consistency.

➢ **Implementing Quality Assurance Measures:**
- Implement quality assurance measures to prevent defects and errors from occurring in the first place. This includes designing robust processes, conducting training programs, and enforcing strict adherence to quality standards.
- Develop quality control checklists, standard operating procedures (SOPs), and inspection protocols to guide employees in performing quality checks and verifying compliance with standards.

➢ **Inspection and Testing:**
- Conduct regular inspections and testing throughout the production or service delivery process to identify any deviations from quality standards. This may involve visual inspections, measurements, sample testing, or performance evaluations.
- Utilize quality control tools and techniques such as statistical process control (SPC), control charts, and Pareto analysis to monitor process variability and detect trends or abnormalities.

➢ **Root Cause Analysis:**
- When quality issues arise, conduct root cause analysis to identify the underlying causes and address them effectively. This involves investigating the factors contributing to defects

or errors and implementing corrective actions to prevent recurrence.

- Encourage a culture of continuous improvement and problem-solving within your organization, where employees are empowered to identify and resolve quality issues proactively.

➢ **Supplier Quality Management:**

- Work closely with suppliers to ensure that raw materials, components, and services meet your quality requirements. Establish clear quality criteria and conduct supplier audits or evaluations to assess compliance with standards.

- Collaborate with suppliers to address any quality issues or concerns promptly, and work together to implement corrective actions and preventive measures.

➢ **Customer Feedback and Complaint Management:**

- Solicit feedback from customers to gauge their satisfaction levels and identify areas for improvement. Implement systems for capturing and addressing customer complaints effectively, and use this feedback to drive continuous improvement initiatives.

- Monitor customer satisfaction metrics, such as Net Promoter Score (NPS) or customer satisfaction surveys, to track performance and identify opportunities for enhancing the quality of products or services.

➢ **Continuous Improvement:**

- Quality control is an ongoing process of continuous improvement. Regularly review and analyze quality performance metrics, identify opportunities for improvement, and implement corrective actions to enhance processes and outcomes.

- Foster a culture of quality excellence within your organization, where every employee is committed to delivering high-quality products or services and continuously striving for improvement.

By prioritizing quality control throughout your business operations, you can build trust with customers, differentiate your brand in the marketplace, and drive long-term success. Invest in robust quality management systems and processes, and make quality a core value that guides every aspect of your business.

Resource Allocation: Maximizing Efficiency and Effectiveness
Resource allocation involves strategically distributing resources such as capital, labor, equipment, and materials to achieve business objectives and maximize productivity. Effective resource allocation is crucial for optimizing efficiency, minimizing waste, and driving sustainable growth. Here's a closer look at the key components of resource allocation:

❖ **Resource Planning:**
- Begin by conducting a comprehensive assessment of your business's resource needs and capabilities. Identify the resources required to support your operations, including human resources, financial resources, physical assets, and technology.
- Develop a resource plan that aligns with your business objectives and production schedules. Consider factors such as demand forecasts, capacity constraints, and budgetary constraints when allocating resources.

❖ **Capacity Planning:**
- Capacity planning involves determining the optimal level of resources needed to meet current and future demand. Assess your business's capacity to produce goods or deliver services and adjust resource allocation accordingly.
- Anticipate fluctuations in demand and plan for scalability to accommodate future growth. This may involve investing in

additional equipment, hiring additional staff, or expanding production facilities as needed.

❖ Resource Optimization:

- Optimize resource utilization to maximize efficiency and minimize waste. Implement best practices and efficiency measures to streamline workflows, reduce downtime, and improve overall productivity.
- Leverage technology and automation to optimize resource allocation and utilization. Utilize software tools and systems that provide real-time visibility into resource availability and performance.

❖ Cross-Training and Skill Development:

- Cross-train employees to perform multiple roles and tasks within your organization. This enhances flexibility and agility, allowing you to adapt to changing business needs and resource constraints.
- Invest in ongoing training and skill development programs to enhance employee competencies and capabilities. Empower your workforce with the knowledge and skills they need to perform their roles effectively and contribute to business success.

❖ Equipment and Asset Management:

- Properly maintain and manage physical assets and equipment to prolong their lifespan and optimize their performance. Implement preventive maintenance schedules and conduct regular inspections to identify and address any issues promptly.
- Utilize asset tracking systems and maintenance management software to monitor equipment usage, track maintenance activities, and optimize asset utilization.

❖ **Financial Resource Management:**
- Manage financial resources effectively to support business operations and strategic initiatives. Develop a budget that allocates funds to key areas such as production, marketing, research and development, and overhead expenses.
- Monitor cash flow and financial performance metrics regularly to ensure that resources are allocated wisely and in accordance with business priorities.

❖ **Risk Assessment and Contingency Planning:**
- Anticipate potential risks and uncertainties that may impact resource availability or utilization. Conduct risk assessments to identify potential threats and develop contingency plans to mitigate their impact.
- Establish backup plans and alternative resource sources to ensure business continuity in the event of unforeseen disruptions or emergencies.

By implementing effective resource allocation strategies, you can optimize efficiency, minimize waste, and maximize the value of your business's resources. Prioritize strategic planning, flexibility, and adaptability to ensure that resources are allocated in a way that supports your business's growth and success.

Risk Management: Navigating Uncertainty for Business Success

Risk management is the process of identifying, assessing, and mitigating potential risks that may impact the success of your business. By proactively managing risks, you can minimize their impact on operations, protect assets, and capitalize on opportunities for growth. Here's a closer look at the key components of risk management:

❖ **Risk Identification:**
- Begin by identifying potential risks that may affect your business, including internal and external factors. Common types of risks include operational risks, financial risks, market risks, regulatory risks, and strategic risks.
- Conduct risk assessments and brainstorming sessions with key stakeholders to identify and prioritize potential threats and opportunities. Consider past experiences, industry trends, and emerging risks when identifying potential hazards.

❖ **Risk Assessment:**
- Assess the likelihood and potential impact of identified risks on your business. Evaluate each risk based on criteria such as probability, severity, and potential consequences.   - Utilize risk assessment tools and techniques such as risk matrices, scenario analysis, and sensitivity analysis to quantify and prioritize risks effectively.

❖ **Risk Mitigation Strategies:**
- Develop risk mitigation strategies to address identified risks and minimize their impact on your business. This may involve implementing preventive measures, controls, or safeguards to reduce the likelihood or severity of risks.
- Consider a combination of risk mitigation strategies, including risk avoidance, risk reduction, risk transfer, and risk acceptance, depending on the nature and severity of the risks.

❖ **Contingency Planning:**
- Develop contingency plans to prepare for and respond to potential risks and crises. Identify alternative courses of action and establish protocols for managing emergencies, disruptions, or adverse events.

- Test contingency plans through simulation exercises or tabletop drills to ensure readiness and effectiveness in real-world scenarios.

❖ **Insurance and Risk Transfer:**
- Consider purchasing insurance coverage to transfer certain types of risks to an insurance provider. Review your business's insurance needs and options, including property insurance, liability insurance, and business interruption insurance.
- Work with insurance brokers or risk management professionals to assess your insurance requirements and identify suitable coverage options that align with your risk management objectives.

❖ **Monitoring and Review:**
- Continuously monitor and review risk factors, performance metrics, and changes in the business environment. Stay informed about emerging risks, regulatory changes, and market trends that may impact your business.
- Conduct regular reviews of your risk management processes and controls to identify areas for improvement and ensure compliance with best practices and regulatory requirements.

❖ **Risk Culture and Governance:**
- Foster a risk-aware culture within your organization, where employees understand their role in identifying and managing risks effectively. Promote open communication, transparency, and accountability regarding risk-related issues.
- Establish clear roles and responsibilities for risk management oversight and governance. Assign accountability for risk management activities to designated individuals or committees within your organization.

By adopting a proactive approach to risk management, you can safeguard your business against potential threats, capitalize on opportunities, and enhance overall resilience and competitiveness. Prioritize risk management as an integral part of your business strategy and decision-making processes to mitigate uncertainty and drive sustainable growth.

Technology Integration: Leveraging Innovation for Business Success

Technology integration involves incorporating digital tools, systems, and solutions into your business operations to enhance efficiency, productivity, and competitiveness. By leveraging technology effectively, you can streamline processes, improve decision-making, and unlock new opportunities for growth. Here's a closer look at the key components of technology integration:

❖ **Automation and Workflow Optimization:**
  - Implement automation technologies to streamline repetitive tasks, reduce manual effort, and improve process efficiency. Automation can help eliminate bottlenecks, minimize errors, and accelerate workflows across various functions within your organization.
  - Identify opportunities for workflow optimization and utilize technology solutions such as workflow management systems, robotic process automation (RPA), and business process management (BPM) tools to standardize and automate processes.

❖ **Data Analytics and Business Intelligence:**
  - Leverage data analytics and business intelligence (BI) tools to gain insights into your business operations, customer behavior, and market trends. Analyze key performance indicators (KPIs), identify patterns and trends, and make data-driven decisions to drive business growth.

- Implement data visualization techniques such as dashboards, reports, and interactive visualizations to communicate insights effectively and facilitate informed decision-making at all levels of the organization.

❖ **Cloud Computing and Software as a Service (SaaS):**
  - Embrace cloud computing technologies to enhance scalability, flexibility, and accessibility in your business operations. Utilize cloud-based software applications and platforms to streamline collaboration, data storage, and IT infrastructure management.
  - Leverage SaaS solutions for functions such as customer relationship management (CRM), enterprise resource planning (ERP), human resource management (HRM), and project management to reduce upfront costs, improve scalability, and stay up-to-date with the latest software updates and features.

❖ **Internet of Things (IoT) Integration:**
  - Explore IoT technologies to connect and integrate physical devices, sensors, and equipment within your business operations. Utilize IoT data to monitor equipment performance, track asset utilization, and optimize resource allocation in real-time.
  - Implement IoT solutions for applications such as predictive maintenance, supply chain visibility, inventory management, and smart facilities management to improve operational efficiency and drive cost savings.

❖ **Digital Marketing and E-commerce Solutions:**
  - Harness digital marketing tools and e-commerce platforms to reach and engage customers more effectively. Utilize search engine optimization (SEO), social media marketing, email marketing, and content marketing strategies to attract and retain customers.

- Invest in e-commerce platforms and online marketplaces to expand your reach, streamline sales processes, and offer customers a convenient and seamless shopping experience across multiple channels and devices.

❖ **Cybersecurity and Data Protection:**
- Prioritize cybersecurity and data protection measures to safeguard sensitive information and mitigate cyber threats. Implement robust security protocols, encryption techniques, and access controls to protect data assets from unauthorized access, breaches, and cyber attacks.
- Stay informed about emerging cybersecurity threats and regulatory requirements, and regularly update security measures to address evolving risks and vulnerabilities.

By integrating technology into your business operations, you can unlock new opportunities for innovation, efficiency, and growth. Embrace digital transformation as a strategic imperative and invest in technologies that align with your business objectives and priorities. With the right technology solutions in place, you can position your business for success in today's rapidly evolving digital landscape.

Customer Relationship Management (CRM): Fostering Loyalty and Satisfaction

Customer relationship management (CRM) is a strategic approach to managing interactions with current and potential customers to foster loyalty, satisfaction, and retention. By implementing CRM strategies and tools, businesses can better understand their customers' needs, personalize interactions, and build long-lasting relationships. Here's a closer look at the key components of CRM:

❖ **Customer Data Management:**
- Centralize customer data from various touchpoints and channels, including sales, marketing, customer service, and

social media. Utilize CRM software to store, organize, and analyze customer information, such as contact details, purchase history, preferences, and interactions.

- Implement data hygiene practices to ensure the accuracy, completeness, and reliability of customer data. Regularly update and cleanse customer records to maintain data integrity and enhance the effectiveness of CRM initiatives.

❖ **Customer Segmentation and Personalization:**

- Segment customers based on characteristics such as demographics, purchase behavior, preferences, and lifecycle stage. Tailor marketing messages, offers, and experiences to specific customer segments to enhance relevance and engagement.
- Leverage CRM tools and automation to deliver personalized communications and recommendations across multiple channels, including email, social media, and website interactions.

❖ **Sales and Opportunity Management:**

- Streamline sales processes and improve sales effectiveness with CRM tools for opportunity management, pipeline tracking, and sales forecasting. Empower sales teams with real-time visibility into customer interactions, sales activities, and deal progress.
- Utilize CRM dashboards and reports to monitor sales performance, track key metrics such as conversion rates and win rates, and identify opportunities for growth and improvement.

❖ **Marketing Automation and Campaign Management:**

- Automate marketing campaigns and workflows to deliver targeted messages and offers to prospects and customers. Use CRM integration with marketing automation platforms to nurture leads, segment audiences, and track campaign performance.

- Leverage CRM data to measure the effectiveness of marketing campaigns, analyze customer engagement, and optimize marketing strategies for better results.

❖ **Customer Service and Support:**

- Provide exceptional customer service and support experiences by integrating CRM with helpdesk and ticketing systems. Enable customer service teams to access customer information, track interactions, and resolve inquiries and issues efficiently.
- Implement self-service options such as knowledge bases, FAQs, and community forums to empower customers to find answers and solutions independently, reducing the burden on support teams.

❖ **Customer Feedback and Satisfaction Measurement:**

- Gather customer feedback through surveys, feedback forms, and social listening tools to understand customer sentiment and satisfaction levels. Use CRM to capture and analyze feedback data, identify trends, and prioritize areas for improvement.
- Monitor key performance indicators (KPIs) such as Net Promoter Score (NPS), customer satisfaction (CSAT), and customer retention rates to gauge overall customer satisfaction and loyalty.

By prioritizing customer relationship management, businesses can strengthen customer loyalty, drive repeat business, and foster advocacy and referrals. Invest in CRM strategies and technologies that align with your business goals and customer-centric values, and prioritize continuous improvement and innovation in customer engagement and satisfaction.

[K]
Legal and Regulatory Compliance: Navigating the Legal Landscape

Starting a business from scratch is an exciting journey filled with opportunities, but it's essential to navigate the legal landscape carefully to ensure compliance with laws and regulations. Understanding and adhering to legal requirements are critical steps in building a solid foundation for your business's success and longevity. In this section, we'll explore key aspects of legal and regulatory compliance to help you navigate the complexities of starting and operating a business responsibly.

Business Structure and Registration: Choosing the Right Path

Selecting the appropriate legal structure for your business is a critical decision that can have far-reaching implications for its success and operations. Beyond determining how your business will be organized legally, the process also involves registering the chosen structure with the relevant government authorities. In this section, we'll explore the importance of understanding both legal structure and business structure, and why they are essential for aspiring entrepreneurs.

❖ **Legal Structure vs. Business Structure: Clarifying Distinctions**

While often used interchangeably, legal structure and business structure refer to different aspects of how a business is organized and operated. Here's a brief overview of the similarities and differences between the two:

Legal Structure: Defining the Framework

The legal structure of a business refers to its formal legal framework, dictating how the business is organized, owned, and operated. It encompasses various forms, including sole proprietorships, partnerships, corporations, and limited liability companies (LLCs). Each legal structure comes with its own set of advantages, disadvantages, and regulatory requirements.

Business Structure: Beyond Legal Framework

Business structure, on the other hand, encompasses more than just the legal aspects. It includes considerations such as operational flexibility, taxation, and liability protection. Business structure decisions can profoundly impact the day-to-day operations, management, and growth potential of a business.

❖ **The Registration Process: Formalizing Your Business**

Regardless of the chosen legal structure, all businesses must undergo the registration process to establish their legal presence and legitimacy. The registration process involves submitting the necessary paperwork and documentation to the appropriate government authorities, such as state agencies or municipal offices. This may include registering your business name, obtaining a tax identification number, and applying for permits or licenses required for your industry and location.

Importance of Understanding Both:

Understanding the distinctions between legal structure and business structure, as well as the registration process, is essential for aspiring entrepreneurs. While the legal structure determines the formal legal framework of the business, the business structure influences its operational dynamics and strategic direction. By comprehensively understanding both aspects, entrepreneurs can make informed decisions that align with their business goals, regulatory requirements, and growth aspirations.

In the following sections, we'll delve deeper into the various business structures available to entrepreneurs and provide guidance on navigating the registration process effectively. By gaining clarity on these fundamental aspects, entrepreneurs can navigate the complexities of starting a business with confidence and clarity.One of the most critical decisions you'll make when starting a business from scratch is choosing the right legal structure and registering your business entity. Your choice of business structure will have significant implications for your business's liability, tax obligations, and operational flexibility. Here's what you need to know to make an informed decision:

1. Sole Proprietorship: Simplicity and Control

A sole proprietorship is the simplest and most common form of business structure, where a single individual owns and operates the business. As a sole proprietor, you have complete control over business decisions and operations. However, you are personally liable for any debts or liabilities incurred by the business, which means your personal assets are at risk if the business faces legal action or financial difficulties.

2. Partnership: Shared Ownership and Responsibility

A partnership is a business structure in which two or more individuals or entities share ownership and management responsibilities. Partnerships can be general partnerships, where all partners have equal liability and responsibility, or limited partnerships, where some partners have limited liability. Partnerships are relatively easy to set up and offer flexibility in management and decision-making. However, partners are jointly liable for the business's debts and obligations, and disagreements among partners can pose challenges.

3. **Corporation: Limited Liability and Separate Legal Entity**

   A corporation is a separate legal entity distinct from its owners (shareholders), offering limited liability protection to its owners. This means that shareholders' personal assets are generally protected from the corporation's debts and liabilities. Corporations have a more complex structure and are subject to more extensive regulatory requirements and formalities, such as holding shareholder meetings, maintaining corporate records, and filing annual reports. However, corporations offer advantages such as perpetual existence, easier access to capital through the sale of stock, and potential tax benefits.

4. **Limited Liability Company (LLC): Flexibility and Liability Protection**

   A limited liability company (LLC) combines the limited liability protection of a corporation with the flexibility and simplicity of a partnership. LLCs offer liability protection for their owners (members) while allowing flexibility in management and taxation. LLCs are not subject to the same formalities and regulatory requirements as corporations, making them easier to set up and maintain. However, LLCs are subject to state-specific regulations, and members may be required to pay self-employment taxes on their share of the company's profits.

Choosing the Right Path: Considerations and Guidance

When choosing the right business structure for your venture, consider factors such as:

➤ **Liability protection:** Do you need personal asset protection from business liabilities?

➤ **Tax implications:** How do different business structures affect your tax obligations and potential tax benefits

➤ **Operational flexibility:** How much control do you want over business decisions and operations?

➢ **Regulatory requirements:** Are you prepared to comply with the formalities and regulations associated with a particular business structure?

It's essential to seek professional advice from attorneys, accountants, or business advisors familiar with your industry and local regulations. They can provide personalized guidance based on your specific circumstances and help you navigate the complexities of business structure selection and registration. Remember that choosing the right business structure is a critical step in laying the foundation for your business's success and growth.By choosing the right business structure, entrepreneurs can lay a solid foundation for their business's success, mitigate risks, and maximize opportunities for growth and innovation.

Aligning Business Structure with Long-Term Goals

Choosing the right business structure is not only about meeting immediate needs but also about positioning the business for long-term success and growth. Aligning the business structure with long-term goals and growth plans is essential for maximizing opportunities, minimizing risks, and ensuring scalability. Here's why it's crucial to consider the long-term implications when selecting a business structure:

✓ **Scalability and Expansion:**
   The business structure you choose can impact your ability to scale and expand your operations over time. Certain structures, such as corporations and LLCs, offer greater flexibility and scalability compared to sole proprietorships and partnerships. They provide mechanisms for raising capital, attracting investors, and expanding into new markets. By selecting a business structure that accommodates future growth, you can position your business for long-term success and expansion.

✓ **Tax Efficiency and Planning:**
Different business structures have varying tax implications for the business and its owners. It's essential to consider how taxation will affect your business's profitability and cash flow, both in the short term and the long term. Working with tax advisors and financial experts can help you develop tax-efficient strategies and take advantage of available tax benefits and incentives. By aligning your business structure with your long-term tax planning goals, you can optimize your tax position and minimize tax liabilities as your business grows.

✓ **Risk Management and Asset Protection:**
Choosing the right business structure can also help mitigate risks and protect personal assets from business liabilities. Structures such as corporations and LLCs offer limited liability protection to their owners, shielding personal assets from business debts and legal claims. This separation between personal and business assets can provide peace of mind and financial security, especially as the business expands and faces increased risks. By structuring your business to minimize exposure to liability, you can safeguard your personal assets and protect your long-term financial interests.

✓ **Succession Planning and Exit Strategies:**
Long-term business success often involves planning for ownership transitions, such as passing the business on to future generations or selling the business outright. The chosen business structure can significantly impact succession planning and exit strategies. For example, corporations may offer more straightforward transferability of ownership through the sale of stock, while partnerships and sole proprietorships may require more complex arrangements. By considering your long-term succession goals and exit strategies upfront, you can

select a business structure that facilitates smooth transitions and maximizes value for stakeholders.

✓ **Regulatory Compliance and Governance:**
As businesses grow and evolve, they may become subject to increasingly complex regulatory requirements and governance standards. Certain business structures, such as corporations, are inherently designed to comply with regulatory mandates and corporate governance practices. By selecting a business structure that aligns with industry regulations and best practices, you can minimize compliance risks and ensure transparency and accountability in your business operations.

Aligning your business structure with long-term goals and growth plans is essential for maximizing opportunities, minimizing risks, and ensuring sustainability. By carefully considering scalability, tax efficiency, risk management, succession planning, and regulatory compliance, you can select a business structure that sets the foundation for long-term success and prosperity.

Impact of Business Structure on Taxation: Maximizing Efficiency and Minimizing Liabilities

The choice of business structure has significant implications for taxation, affecting both the business itself and its owners. Understanding how different structures are taxed can help entrepreneurs make informed decisions that optimize tax efficiency and minimize liabilities. In this section, we'll explore how various business structures impact taxation and considerations for maximizing tax benefits.

✓ **Sole Proprietorship: Pass-Through Taxation and Self-Employment Taxes**
In a sole proprietorship, the business and the owner are considered the same legal entity for tax purposes. Income and

expenses from the business are reported on the owner's personal tax return using Schedule C (Form 1040). Sole proprietors are subject to self-employment taxes, which include both the employee and employer portions of Social Security and Medicare taxes. While sole proprietors benefit from simplicity and flexibility, they are taxed at individual income tax rates, which can be higher than corporate tax rates.

✓ **Partnership: Pass-Through Taxation and Distribution of Profits**

Partnerships, including general partnerships, limited partnerships, and limited liability partnerships (LLPs), are pass-through entities, meaning that profits and losses are passed through to the partners and reported on their individual tax returns. Partnerships do not pay income taxes at the entity level. Instead, partners pay taxes on their share of partnership income based on their ownership percentage. Partnerships offer flexibility in allocating profits and losses among partners, allowing for tax planning strategies to maximize tax benefits.

✓ **Corporation: Double Taxation and Corporate Income Taxes**

Corporations are taxed separately from their owners, resulting in potential double taxation. Corporations pay corporate income taxes on their profits at the corporate tax rate, and shareholders pay taxes on dividends received from the corporation at individual tax rates. This double taxation can lead to higher overall tax liabilities for both the corporation and its shareholders. However, corporations may benefit from lower corporate tax rates, tax-deferred savings opportunities, and deductions for business expenses.

✓ **Limited Liability Company (LLC): Flexibility in Taxation**

Limited liability companies (LLCs) offer flexibility in taxation, allowing owners (members) to choose how they want to be taxed. By default, LLCs are taxed as pass-through entities, similar to partnerships, with profits and losses passed through to the members' personal tax returns. However, LLCs can elect to be taxed as a corporation (either as a C corporation or an S corporation) to take advantage of corporate tax rates, tax-deferred savings, and other tax benefits. This flexibility allows LLCs to tailor their tax treatment to suit their specific circumstances and tax planning goals.

Considerations for Maximizing Tax Benefits

When selecting a business structure, entrepreneurs should consider several factors to maximize tax benefits and minimize liabilities:

- **Business Goals and Growth Plans:**
  Choose a structure that aligns with your long-term business goals and growth plans, considering factors such as scalability, access to capital, and exit strategies.
- **Tax Efficiency:**
  Evaluate the tax implications of each structure and consider the most tax-efficient option based on your anticipated income, expenses, and deductions.
- **Risk Management:**
  Balance tax considerations with liability protection and risk management strategies to safeguard personal assets and minimize exposure to legal and financial risks.
- **Regulatory Compliance:**
  Ensure compliance with tax laws and regulations, and work with tax advisors and financial experts to implement tax-efficient strategies and maximize available tax benefits.

By carefully considering the tax implications of different business structures and implementing tax-efficient strategies, entrepreneurs can optimize their tax position, reduce tax liabilities, and retain more of their hard-earned profits.

Licensing and Permits: Meeting Regulatory Requirements

Obtaining the necessary licenses and permits is a fundamental aspect of legal and regulatory compliance for businesses across various industries. These licenses and permits are required to operate legally, ensure public safety, protect the environment, and maintain the integrity of the marketplace. In this section, we'll explore the importance of licensing and permits and provide guidance on navigating the regulatory landscape effectively.

❖ **Ensuring Legal Compliance:**
Obtaining the appropriate licenses and permits is essential for ensuring legal compliance and avoiding regulatory violations that could result in fines, penalties, or even business closure. Regulatory agencies at the federal, state, and local levels oversee licensing and permitting requirements for different industries, ranging from healthcare and construction to food service and manufacturing. By understanding and fulfilling these requirements, businesses demonstrate their commitment to operating responsibly and ethically within the confines of the law.

❖ **Protecting Public Health and Safety:**
Many licensing and permitting requirements are designed to protect public health and safety by ensuring that businesses meet specific standards and regulations. For example, restaurants may need health permits to ensure food safety and sanitation, while construction companies may require permits to comply with building codes and regulations. By obtaining the necessary licenses and permits, businesses demonstrate their commitment to maintaining high standards of quality, safety, and integrity in their operations, thereby safeguarding public health and safety.

❖ **Preserving Environmental Quality:**
Businesses engaged in activities with environmental implications, such as manufacturing, construction, and waste management, may need permits to comply with environmental regulations and protect natural resources. Environmental permits may be required for activities such as air emissions, wastewater discharge, hazardous waste management, and land development. By obtaining these permits and adhering to environmental standards, businesses minimize their impact on the environment and contribute to sustainable development and conservation efforts.

❖ **Promoting Consumer Confidence:**
Licensing and permitting requirements also play a crucial role in promoting consumer confidence and trust in businesses. Consumers expect businesses to operate legally, ethically, and responsibly, and compliance with licensing and permitting regulations helps reinforce this trust. Businesses that hold valid licenses and permits signal to consumers that they have met regulatory standards, undergone necessary inspections, and are committed to delivering quality products and services in a safe and transparent manner. This, in turn, enhances brand reputation, fosters customer loyalty, and drives business growth.

❖ **Navigating the Regulatory Landscape:**
Navigating the complex regulatory landscape of licensing and permitting can be challenging for businesses, especially those operating in highly regulated industries or across multiple jurisdictions. It's essential for businesses to conduct thorough research, identify applicable licensing and permitting requirements, and proactively engage with regulatory authorities to ensure compliance. Seeking assistance from

legal advisors, industry associations, or consulting firms specializing in regulatory compliance can provide valuable guidance and support in navigating the regulatory landscape effectively.

Conclusion: Meeting Regulatory Requirements with Licensing and Permits

Obtaining the necessary licenses and permits is a critical component of legal and regulatory compliance for businesses. By ensuring legal compliance, protecting public health and safety, preserving environmental quality, promoting consumer confidence, and navigating the regulatory landscape effectively, businesses can demonstrate their commitment to responsible and ethical business practices. Investing time, resources, and effort into obtaining and maintaining licenses and permits is not only a legal requirement but also a strategic imperative for long-term success and sustainability.

Tax Compliance: Fulfilling Your Tax Obligations

Complying with tax laws and regulations is a fundamental responsibility for businesses of all sizes and structures. Failure to meet tax obligations can result in severe consequences, including fines, penalties, and legal actions. In this section, we'll explore the importance of tax compliance and provide guidance on navigating the complex landscape of business taxation effectively.

❖ **Legal Obligation and Accountability:**
   Businesses have a legal obligation to comply with tax laws and regulations at the federal, state, and local levels. Failure to fulfill tax obligations can lead to serious consequences, including audits, investigations, and legal actions by tax authorities. By prioritizing tax compliance, businesses demonstrate their commitment to operating lawfully and ethically, thereby

avoiding costly penalties and preserving their reputation and credibility.

❖ Financial Stability and Sustainability:

Maintaining tax compliance is essential for ensuring financial stability and sustainability for businesses. Taxes are a significant expense for businesses, and non-compliance can disrupt cash flow, erode profitability, and undermine long-term viability. By accurately calculating and timely paying taxes, businesses can manage their financial obligations effectively, avoid unnecessary financial strain, and maintain a solid foundation for growth and success.

❖ Building Trust with Stakeholders:

Tax compliance is not only a legal requirement but also a key component of corporate governance and transparency. Businesses that demonstrate a commitment to tax compliance build trust and confidence with stakeholders,
including customers, investors, creditors, and regulatory authorities. Transparent tax practices enhance credibility, reduce reputational risks, and foster stronger relationships with stakeholders, contributing to long-term business success and sustainability.

❖ Mitigating Risks and Liabilities:

Non-compliance with tax laws and regulations exposes businesses to various risks and liabilities, including financial penalties, interest charges, and legal actions. Tax authorities have the power to impose severe penalties for tax evasion, fraud, or negligence, which can have far-reaching consequences for businesses and their owners. By proactively addressing tax compliance issues, businesses can mitigate risks, avoid potential liabilities, and protect their financial interests and assets.

❖ **Leveraging Tax Planning Opportunities:**
While tax compliance involves fulfilling tax obligations, businesses can also leverage tax planning opportunities to minimize tax liabilities legally. Strategic tax planning allows businesses to optimize their tax position, take advantage of available deductions and credits, and maximize tax savings. By working with tax advisors and financial experts, businesses can develop tax-efficient strategies tailored to their specific circumstances and objectives, thereby enhancing their financial performance and competitiveness.

Conclusion: Fulfilling Tax Obligations with Compliance

Tax compliance is a critical aspect of responsible and ethical business conduct. By fulfilling tax obligations, businesses uphold their legal and ethical responsibilities, maintain financial stability and sustainability, build trust with stakeholders, mitigate risks and liabilities, and leverage tax planning opportunities for long-term success and prosperity. Investing in tax compliance not only ensures regulatory compliance but also contributes to the overall integrity, credibility, and resilience of businesses in today's competitive marketplace.

Intellectual Property Protection: Safeguarding Your Assets

Intellectual property (IP) refers to creations of the mind, such as inventions, literary and artistic works, designs, symbols, names, and images used in commerce. Protecting intellectual property is crucial for businesses to maintain their competitive advantage, preserve innovation, and safeguard valuable assets. In this section, we'll explore the importance of intellectual property protection and provide guidance on securing and managing intellectual property assets effectively.

❖ **Preserving Innovation and Creativity:**
Intellectual property protection encourages innovation and creativity by providing creators and inventors with exclusive rights to their creations. Patents protect inventions, copyrights protect original works of authorship, trademarks protect brands and logos, and trade secrets protect valuable business information. By securing intellectual property rights, businesses can invest in research and development, create new products and services, and differentiate themselves in the marketplace, driving innovation and economic growth.

❖ **Maintaining Competitive Advantage:**
Intellectual property assets are often a source of competitive advantage for businesses, distinguishing them from competitors and enhancing their market position. Trademarks enable businesses to build brand recognition and loyalty among customers, while patents protect inventions from being copied or replicated by competitors. By protecting their intellectual property, businesses can maintain their market share, attract customers, and command premium prices for their products and services, thereby securing a competitive edge in the marketplace.

❖ **Enhancing Marketability and Valuation:**
Intellectual property assets can significantly enhance the marketability and valuation of businesses, particularly in industries where innovation and intangible assets play a significant role. Investors, lenders, and potential partners often assess a company's intellectual property portfolio as part of their due diligence process. A strong portfolio of patents, trademarks, copyrights, and trade secrets can increase the attractiveness of a business to investors and enhance its overall

valuation, leading to potential opportunities for funding, partnerships, and strategic alliances.

❖ **Protecting Brand Reputation and Integrity:**
Intellectual property protection is essential for safeguarding brand reputation and integrity in the marketplace. Trademarks protect brands from infringement and counterfeiting, ensuring that consumers can trust the quality and authenticity of products and services. Copyrights protect original creative works from unauthorized use or reproduction, preserving the integrity of artistic expressions and cultural heritage. By protecting their intellectual property rights, businesses uphold their brand reputation, maintain consumer trust, and avoid reputational damage resulting from IP infringement or misappropriation.

❖ **Mitigating Risks and Legal Liabilities:**
Failure to protect intellectual property rights can expose businesses to various risks and legal liabilities, including infringement lawsuits, loss of market share, and damage to brand reputation. Intellectual property infringement can result in costly litigation, financial damages, and injunctions that restrict business operations. By proactively securing and enforcing their intellectual property rights, businesses can mitigate these risks, deter potential infringers, and protect their investment in innovation and creativity.

Conclusion: Safeguarding Your Intellectual Property Assets
Intellectual property protection is a critical component of business strategy and risk management. By preserving innovation, maintaining competitive advantage, enhancing marketability and valuation, protecting brand reputation and integrity, and mitigating risks and legal liabilities, businesses can safeguard their

intellectual property assets and maximize their value and impact in the marketplace. Investing in intellectual property protection not only protects business interests but also fosters innovation, creativity, and economic growth in today's knowledge-driven economy.

Employment Laws and Regulations: Prioritizing Fair Treatment
Compliance with employment laws and regulations is essential for businesses to create a fair and inclusive workplace, protect employee rights, and minimize legal risks. Employment laws govern various aspects of the employer-employee relationship, including recruitment, hiring, compensation, benefits, working conditions, and termination. In this section, we'll explore the importance of compliance with employment laws and regulations and provide guidance on promoting fair treatment and legal compliance in the workplace.

❖ **Ensuring Fair and Equal Treatment:**
Compliance with employment laws and regulations is crucial for ensuring fair and equal treatment of employees regardless of their race, gender, age, disability, religion, or other protected characteristics. Anti-discrimination laws, such as Title VII of the Civil Rights Act, the Americans with Disabilities Act (ADA), and the Age Discrimination in Employment Act (ADEA), prohibit discrimination in hiring, promotion, compensation, and other employment practices. By adhering to these laws, businesses create a workplace culture that values diversity, promotes inclusivity, and fosters a sense of belonging among employees.

❖ **Protecting Employee Rights and Benefits:**
Employment laws and regulations also protect employee rights and benefits, such as minimum wage, overtime pay, meal and rest breaks, family and medical leave, and workplace safety. Laws such as the Fair Labor Standards Act (FLSA), the Family

and Medical Leave Act (FMLA), and the Occupational Safety and Health Act (OSHA) establish standards for wages, hours, and working conditions to ensure the health, safety, and well-being of employees. Compliance with these laws helps businesses meet their legal obligations, uphold employee rights, and maintain a positive and productive work environment.

- ❖ **Preventing Harassment and Workplace Misconduct:**
  Employment laws and regulations include provisions aimed at preventing harassment, bullying, and other forms of workplace misconduct. Laws such as Title VII and the Equal Employment Opportunity Commission (EEOC) guidelines prohibit harassment based on protected characteristics, such as race, gender, religion, and sexual orientation. Employers are responsible for creating a work environment free from harassment and taking prompt and effective action to address complaints and allegations of misconduct. By enforcing anti-harassment policies and providing training and resources to employees, businesses can foster a respectful and inclusive workplace culture.

- ❖ **Complying with Employment Documentation and Recordkeeping:**
  Employment laws and regulations require businesses to maintain accurate and up-to-date documentation and records related to employment matters, including hiring, payroll, benefits, performance evaluations, and disciplinary actions. Compliance with recordkeeping requirements ensures transparency, accountability, and compliance with legal obligations. Employers must keep records for specified periods as required by law and make them available for inspection by regulatory agencies or in response to legal inquiries or disputes.

❖ **Navigating Evolving Legal Landscape:**
Employment laws and regulations are subject to frequent changes and updates in response to shifting social, economic, and political dynamics. Businesses must stay informed about new laws, regulations, and court decisions affecting the employer-employee relationship and adjust their policies and practices accordingly. Proactive engagement with legal counsel, human resources professionals, and industry associations can help businesses navigate the evolving legal landscape, anticipate compliance challenges, and implement effective strategies to ensure legal compliance and fair treatment in the workplace.

Conclusion: Prioritizing Fair Treatment and Legal Compliance

Compliance with employment laws and regulations is essential for businesses to create a fair, inclusive, and legally compliant workplace. By ensuring fair and equal treatment, protecting employee rights and benefits, preventing harassment and workplace misconduct, complying with employment documentation and recordkeeping requirements, and navigating the evolving legal landscape, businesses can prioritize fair treatment and legal compliance while fostering a positive and productive work environment for all employees.

Data Privacy and Security: Safeguarding Sensitive Information

In today's digital age, businesses collect, store, and process vast amounts of sensitive information, including customer data, financial records, and proprietary business information. Protecting this data from unauthorized access, breaches, and misuse is essential for maintaining trust, complying with regulations, and safeguarding business reputation. In this section, we'll explore the importance of data privacy and security and provide guidance on implementing robust measures to protect sensitive information effectively.

❖ **Protecting Customer Trust and Confidence:**
Data privacy and security are paramount for protecting customer trust and confidence in businesses. Customers expect businesses to handle their personal information responsibly and securely, safeguarding it from unauthorized access, breaches, and misuse. By implementing robust data privacy and security measures, businesses demonstrate their commitment to protecting customer privacy, maintaining confidentiality, and upholding ethical standards in data handling practices.

❖ **Complying with Data Protection Regulations:**
Businesses are subject to various data protection regulations and laws designed to safeguard individuals' privacy and personal information. Regulations such as the General Data Protection Regulation (GDPR) in the European Union and the California Consumer Privacy Act (CCPA) in the United States establish strict requirements for data collection, processing, storage, and disclosure. Compliance with these regulations requires businesses to implement measures such as data encryption, access controls, data minimization, and privacy policies to protect sensitive information and ensure transparency and accountability in data handling practices.

❖ **Mitigating Risks of Data Breaches and Cyberattacks:**
Data breaches and cyberattacks pose significant risks to businesses, including financial losses, reputational damage, and legal liabilities. Hackers and cybercriminals target businesses to steal sensitive information, such as customer data, financial records, and trade secrets, for illicit purposes, such as identity theft, fraud, and corporate espionage. By implementing robust cybersecurity measures, such as firewalls, antivirus software, intrusion detection systems, and

employee training programs, businesses can mitigate the risks of data breaches and cyberattacks and protect sensitive information from unauthorized access and exploitation.

❖ **Ensuring Business Continuity and Resilience:**
Data privacy and security are essential for ensuring business continuity and resilience in the face of unforeseen events, such as natural disasters, technological failures, or malicious attacks. Businesses rely on data to support critical operations, make informed decisions, and deliver products and services to customers. By implementing data backup and recovery plans, disaster recovery strategies, and incident response protocols, businesses can minimize disruptions, recover quickly from data breaches or cyberattacks, and maintain continuity of operations, thereby preserving their reputation and credibility in the marketplace.

❖ **Fostering a Culture of Data Privacy and Security:**
Data privacy and security are not just technical or operational concerns but also cultural and organizational imperatives. Businesses must foster a culture of data privacy and security among employees, emphasizing the importance of responsible data handling practices, confidentiality, and compliance with policies and procedures. Employee training and awareness programs play a critical role in educating staff about data privacy risks, best practices, and their role in safeguarding sensitive information, thereby empowering them to become proactive stewards of data privacy and security within the organization.

Conclusion: Safeguarding Sensitive Information with Data Privacy and Security

Data privacy and security are essential for protecting sensitive information, maintaining trust with customers, complying with regulations, and preserving business reputation and credibility. By prioritizing data privacy and security, businesses can mitigate the risks of data breaches and cyberattacks, comply with data protection regulations, ensure business continuity and resilience, and foster a culture of responsible data handling practices. Investing in robust data privacy and security measures is not only a legal and ethical obligation but also a strategic imperative for businesses to thrive in today's interconnected and data-driven world.

Industry-Specific Regulations: Navigating Sector-Specific Requirements

Industry-specific regulations play a crucial role in governing businesses operating in various sectors, ensuring compliance with standards tailored to their unique characteristics and risks. Navigating these sector-specific requirements effectively is essential for businesses to mitigate risks, ensure compliance, and maintain competitiveness. In this section, we'll explore strategies for navigating industry-specific regulations and achieving regulatory compliance in different sectors.

❖ **Understanding Sector-Specific Regulations:**

The first step in navigating industry-specific regulations is to gain a thorough understanding of the regulatory landscape governing the sector in which the business operates. This involves identifying relevant laws, regulations, guidelines, and industry standards applicable to the business activities and products/services offered. Businesses should conduct comprehensive research, consult legal experts, and engage with industry associations to stay informed about sector-specific regulations and compliance requirements.

❖ **Conducting Compliance Assessments:**
Once businesses have identified sector-specific regulations, they should conduct compliance assessments to evaluate their current practices and identify areas of non-compliance or potential risks. Compliance assessments involve reviewing policies, procedures, operations, and systems to ensure alignment with regulatory requirements. Businesses may need to conduct internal audits, risk assessments, and gap analyses to identify areas for improvement and develop action plans to address compliance deficiencies proactively.

❖ **Implementing Robust Compliance Programs:**
To navigate industry-specific regulations effectively, businesses should implement robust compliance programs tailored to their sector's requirements and risk profiles. Compliance programs should include policies, procedures, controls, and training programs designed to promote awareness, accountability, and adherence to regulatory requirements. Businesses should appoint compliance officers or teams responsible for overseeing compliance efforts, monitoring regulatory developments, and implementing corrective actions as needed.

❖ **Engaging with Regulatory Authorities:**
Building constructive relationships with regulatory authorities and stakeholders is essential for navigating industry-specific regulations successfully. Businesses should proactively engage with regulatory agencies, industry regulators, and trade associations to seek guidance, clarify regulatory requirements, and address compliance-related concerns. Open

communication, transparency, and cooperation with regulatory authorities can help businesses demonstrate their commitment to compliance and resolve issues effectively.

❖ **Investing in Technology and Innovation:**
Technology and innovation can play a significant role in facilitating compliance with industry-specific regulations. Businesses can leverage technology solutions, such as regulatory compliance software, data analytics tools, and automation platforms, to streamline compliance processes, monitor regulatory changes, and ensure timely reporting and documentation. Investing in innovative technologies can help businesses adapt to evolving regulatory requirements, enhance operational efficiency, and maintain a competitive edge in their respective industries.

❖ **Monitoring and Adapting to Regulatory Changes:**
Industry-specific regulations are subject to frequent changes and updates in response to emerging trends, technological advancements, and regulatory developments. Businesses must stay vigilant and proactive in monitoring regulatory changes, analyzing their potential impact, and adapting their compliance strategies accordingly. Establishing mechanisms for tracking regulatory updates, conducting regular compliance reviews, and engaging in industry forums and discussions can help businesses stay ahead of regulatory changes and maintain compliance effectively.

Conclusion: Navigating Industry-Specific Regulations
Navigating industry-specific regulations requires a proactive and systematic approach, grounded in a deep understanding of sector-specific requirements and risks. By understanding regulations, conducting compliance assessments, implementing robust

compliance programs, engaging with regulatory authorities, investing in technology and innovation, and monitoring regulatory changes, businesses can navigate industry-specific regulations effectively, mitigate risks, and ensure compliance with regulatory requirements. Proactive compliance efforts not only protect businesses from legal and financial liabilities but also foster trust, credibility, and sustainability in today's highly regulated business environment.

Embracing Innovation: Fostering Creativity and Adaptability

Innovation lies at the heart of entrepreneurship, driving the creation of new products, services, and business models that disrupt markets, solve customer problems, and fuel growth. Embracing innovation is essential for businesses starting from scratch to differentiate themselves, seize opportunities, and navigate challenges effectively. In this section, we'll explore the importance of embracing innovation and provide guidance on fostering creativity and adaptability in the entrepreneurial journey.

❖ **Driving Business Differentiation:**

Innovation allows businesses to differentiate themselves from competitors by offering unique value propositions, innovative solutions, and exceptional customer experiences. Whether through product innovation, process innovation, or business model innovation, embracing creativity and innovation enables businesses to carve out their niche in the market, attract customers, and build brand loyalty. By continuously innovating and evolving, businesses can stay ahead of the competition and maintain relevance in dynamic and competitive market environments.

❖ **Solving Customer Problems:**

Successful businesses start by identifying and solving customer problems or addressing unmet needs effectively. Embracing innovation enables entrepreneurs to develop innovative solutions that address customer pain points, enhance convenience, and improve quality of life. By understanding customer needs, preferences, and behaviors, businesses can innovate products, services, and experiences that resonate with their target audience, drive customer satisfaction, and foster long-term relationships. Customer-centric innovation is key to building a sustainable and customer-focused business model from scratch.

❖ **Adapting to Market Dynamics:**
The business landscape is constantly evolving, shaped by technological advancements, changing consumer preferences, regulatory developments, and competitive pressures. Embracing innovation allows businesses to adapt to market dynamics, anticipate trends, and pivot their strategies accordingly. Entrepreneurs starting from scratch must embrace a mindset of agility and adaptability, continuously scanning the environment for opportunities and threats, experimenting with new ideas and approaches, and iterating based on feedback and learnings.

❖ **Fostering a Culture of Creativity and Experimentation:**
Creating a culture that values creativity, experimentation, and risk-taking is essential for fostering innovation within the organization. Entrepreneurs should encourage employees to think creatively, challenge conventional wisdom, and explore new possibilities. Providing resources, support, and incentives for innovation, such as dedicated time for brainstorming sessions, innovation workshops, and rewards for successful ideas, can cultivate a culture of innovation that drives business growth and success from the ground up.

❖ **Leveraging Technology and Digital Transformation:**
Technology plays a pivotal role in driving innovation and digital transformation in today's business landscape. Entrepreneurs starting from scratch can leverage technology to streamline operations, enhance customer experiences, and unlock new opportunities for growth. Embracing emerging technologies, such as artificial intelligence, machine learning, blockchain, and the Internet of Things (IoT), allows businesses to innovate across various aspects of their operations, from product development and marketing to supply chain management and customer service.

Conclusion: Embracing Innovation for Business Success
Embracing innovation is essential for entrepreneurs starting a business from scratch to differentiate themselves, solve customer problems, adapt to market dynamics, and drive sustainable growth and success. By fostering a culture of creativity and experimentation, leveraging technology and digital transformation, and continuously seeking opportunities for innovation, entrepreneurs can build resilient and adaptable businesses that thrive in today's rapidly changing business environment. Embracing innovation is not just about creating something new but also about challenging the status quo, pushing boundaries, and shaping the future of business.

[L]
Focus on Customer Service: Building Relationships and Satisfaction

Customer service is a cornerstone of business success, particularly for startups aiming to establish a strong foundation and loyal customer base. Prioritizing excellent customer service helps businesses differentiate themselves, build trust, and foster long-term relationships with customers. In this section, we'll explore the importance of focusing on customer service and provide guidance on delivering exceptional experiences to customers from the outset of starting a business.

❖ **Understanding Customer Needs and Expectations:**
Customers have diverse needs, preferences, and expectations when interacting with businesses. Startups must conduct thorough market research to understand their target audience and gather insights into what drives their purchasing decisions. This involves analyzing demographic data, studying consumer behavior trends, and identifying pain points or challenges that customers face. By gaining a deep understanding of their customers, startups can tailor their products, services, and customer interactions to meet and exceed expectations effectively.

❖ **Providing Personalized and Responsive Support:**
In today's fast-paced business environment, customers expect timely and personalized support when they encounter issues or have questions about products or services. Startups should invest in customer service channels that enable them to deliver responsive support, such as phone support, email support, live chat, and social media. Customer service representatives should be trained to empathize with customers, actively listen

to their concerns, and offer personalized solutions that address their specific needs. Providing personalized and responsive support enhances the overall customer experience and strengthens customer satisfaction and loyalty.

❖ **Building Trust and Credibility:**
Trust is a fundamental component of customer relationships. Startups must prioritize transparency, honesty, and integrity in their interactions with customers to build trust and credibility over time. This involves delivering on promises, being transparent about product features and pricing, and taking responsibility for any mistakes or shortcomings. By building trust and credibility, startups can foster positive relationships with customers, encourage repeat business, and generate positive word-of-mouth referrals, which are crucial for business growth and success.

❖ **Soliciting and Acting on Customer Feedback:**
Customer feedback is invaluable for startups seeking to improve their products, services, and customer experiences. Startups should actively solicit feedback from customers through surveys, reviews, and feedback forms, and use this input to identify areas for improvement and implement changes accordingly. Acting on customer feedback demonstrates responsiveness and a commitment to customer satisfaction, ultimately leading to higher levels of customer loyalty and advocacy. Startups should view customer feedback as an opportunity for growth and innovation, leveraging it to refine their offerings and better meet customer needs.

❖ **Embracing Technology for Enhanced Customer Service:**
Technology can be a powerful enabler of exceptional customer service. Startups can leverage technology solutions such as

customer relationship management (CRM) systems, helpdesk software, and artificial intelligence (AI)-powered chatbots to streamline customer interactions and provide personalized support at scale. These tools enable startups to automate routine tasks, track customer interactions, and provide consistent support across multiple channels. By embracing technology, startups can enhance efficiency, reduce response times, and deliver seamless customer experiences that drive satisfaction and loyalty.

Focusing on customer service excellence is essential for startups to build strong customer relationships, differentiate themselves in the marketplace, and drive long-term success and growth. By understanding customer needs and expectations, providing personalized and responsive support, building trust and credibility, soliciting and acting on customer feedback, and embracing technology for enhanced customer service, startups can create memorable experiences that delight customers and set the stage for sustainable business success. Prioritizing customer service from the outset is not just about satisfying customers but also about building lasting relationships and fostering a loyal customer base that fuels business growth and prosperity.

[M]
Manage Finances Effectively: Navigating Financial Challenges

Managing finances effectively is essential for the success and sustainability of any business, especially for startups facing the challenges of establishing themselves in the market. From budgeting and cash flow management to financial forecasting and investment decisions, startups must prioritize sound financial management practices to ensure long-term viability and growth. In this section, we'll explore the importance of managing finances effectively and provide guidance on navigating financial challenges in the entrepreneurial journey.

✓ **Budgeting and Financial Planning:**
Budgeting and financial planning are foundational elements of effective financial management for startups. Establishing a realistic budget that accounts for startup costs, operational expenses, and revenue projections allows startups to allocate resources efficiently and monitor financial performance. Financial planning involves setting clear financial goals, developing strategies to achieve them, and regularly reviewing and adjusting plans based on changing circumstances. By creating a solid financial plan, startups can make informed decisions, prioritize spending, and stay on track to achieve their objectives.

✓ **Cash Flow Management:**
Cash flow management is critical for startups to maintain liquidity and meet financial obligations in a timely manner. Startups must carefully monitor cash inflows and outflows, anticipate cash flow gaps, and implement strategies to manage working capital effectively. This may involve negotiating

favorable payment terms with suppliers, optimizing inventory levels, and implementing efficient invoicing and collection processes. By maintaining positive cash flow, startups can avoid cash shortages, minimize reliance on external financing, and ensure financial stability and resilience in the face of unexpected challenges.

✓ **Financial Forecasting and Analysis:**
Financial forecasting and analysis enable startups to anticipate future financial performance, identify trends, and make informed business decisions. Startups should regularly analyze financial data, such as sales forecasts, expense trends, and profitability metrics, to gain insights into their financial health and performance. This analysis can help startups identify areas for improvement, optimize resource allocation, and capitalize on growth opportunities. By leveraging financial forecasting and analysis, startups can make strategic decisions that drive profitability and sustainable growth over time.

✓ **Investment and Capital Allocation:**
Startups must carefully consider their investment decisions and allocate capital wisely to maximize returns and minimize risks. Whether it's investing in product development, marketing initiatives, or infrastructure upgrades, startups should evaluate potential investments based on their alignment with business goals, expected returns, and risk profiles. Startups should also explore various sources of funding, such as equity financing, debt financing, or alternative financing options, and choose the most suitable options based on their capital needs and growth plans. By making strategic investment decisions and allocating capital efficiently, startups can optimize their financial resources and drive long-term value creation.

✓ **Risk Management and Contingency Planning:**
Risk management is integral to effective financial management for startups, helping mitigate potential threats and safeguard against financial losses. Startups should identify and assess key risks, such as market risks, operational risks, and regulatory risks, and develop contingency plans to mitigate these risks effectively. This may involve diversifying revenue streams, purchasing insurance coverage, or establishing emergency funds to address unforeseen challenges. By proactively managing risks and preparing for contingencies, startups can enhance their resilience and adaptability, ensuring financial stability and sustainability in the face of uncertainty.

✓ **Cost Control and Expense Management:**
Cost control and expense management are crucial for startups to optimize operational efficiency and preserve financial resources. Startups should regularly review their expenses, identify cost-saving opportunities, and implement measures to reduce unnecessary spending. This may involve negotiating lower vendor prices, outsourcing non-core functions, or implementing cost-effective alternatives. By controlling costs and managing expenses effectively, startups can improve profitability and allocate resources more strategically.

✓ **Pricing Strategy and Revenue Optimization:**
Pricing strategy plays a significant role in determining the profitability and sustainability of startups. Startups must carefully assess market dynamics, competitive pricing, and customer value perception to set optimal prices for their products or services. This involves conducting pricing analyses, experimenting with different pricing models, and adjusting prices based on market feedback and performance metrics. By

optimizing pricing strategies, startups can maximize revenue generation, enhance profitability, and maintain competitiveness in the market.

✓ **Financial Reporting and Performance Monitoring:**
Financial reporting and performance monitoring are essential for startups to track their financial health and make informed business decisions. Startups should establish robust accounting systems and procedures to accurately record financial transactions, generate timely financial statements, and comply with regulatory requirements. Regular financial reporting allows startups to assess their financial performance, identify trends, and measure progress against key performance indicators (KPIs). By monitoring financial performance closely, startups can identify areas for improvement and make adjustments to achieve their financial goals more effectively.

✓ **Debt Management and Financing Strategies:**
Debt management is critical for startups seeking to optimize their capital structure and minimize financial risks. Startups should carefully evaluate their financing options, including debt financing, equity financing, and alternative financing sources, and choose the most appropriate financing strategies based on their growth objectives and risk tolerance. This may involve negotiating favorable loan terms, managing debt repayment schedules, and diversifying sources of funding to reduce reliance on any single source. By effectively managing debt and financing, startups can strengthen their financial position and support sustainable growth.

✓ **Tax Planning and Compliance:**
Tax planning and compliance are essential aspects of financial management for startups to ensure regulatory compliance and minimize tax liabilities. Startups should develop tax planning strategies that optimize tax efficiency, maximize available deductions and credits, and mitigate tax risks. This may involve consulting with tax professionals, staying informed about tax laws and regulations, and maintaining accurate financial records to support tax filings. By proactively managing tax obligations, startups can minimize financial surprises, avoid penalties, and preserve cash flow for business growth and development.

Conclusion: Strengthening Financial Management for Startup Success

Managing finances effectively is critical for startup success, requiring careful planning, discipline, and strategic decision-making. By prioritizing cost control and expense management, optimizing pricing strategies, implementing robust financial reporting systems, managing debt and financing wisely, and ensuring tax compliance, startups can strengthen their financial management practices and position themselves for long-term success and growth. Effective financial management is essential for startups to navigate challenges, seize opportunities, and achieve their business objectives in today's dynamic and competitive business environment.

[N]
Cultivate a Supportive Network: Building Relationships and Partnerships

"Cultivate a Supportive Network" refers to the importance of building and nurturing relationships with various individuals and organizations that can provide valuable support, guidance, and opportunities for startups. Cultivating a supportive network involves actively seeking out mentors, advisors, peers, investors, and industry partners who can offer insights, expertise, resources, and connections to help startups overcome challenges and achieve their goals.

Building a supportive network is essential for startups to gain access to resources, expertise, and opportunities that can fuel their growth and success. By forging meaningful relationships with mentors, advisors, peers, investors, and industry partners, startups can tap into a wealth of knowledge, experience, and support that can help them overcome challenges and navigate the complexities of starting and scaling a business. In this section, we'll explore the importance of cultivating a supportive network and provide guidance on building and nurturing relationships that can drive startup success.

Now, let's delve into the specific points within this topic:

Mentors and Advisors:
Mentors and advisors play a pivotal role in providing guidance, insights, and support to startups as they navigate the entrepreneurial journey. Startups should seek out mentors and advisors who have relevant industry experience, expertise, and networks that can help them overcome challenges and make informed decisions. Building strong relationships with mentors and advisors involves seeking their advice, actively listening to

their feedback, and leveraging their networks and connections to open doors to new opportunities. By cultivating mentorship relationships, startups can gain valuable perspective, avoid common pitfalls, and accelerate their growth trajectory.

Peer Networks and Communities:
Connecting with fellow entrepreneurs and building relationships within peer networks and communities can provide startups with a sense of camaraderie, support, and collaboration. Joining startup accelerators, incubators, networking groups, and online communities allows startups to exchange ideas, share experiences, and learn from each other's successes and failures. Peer networks provide opportunities for networking, collaboration, and peer-to-peer learning, fostering a supportive ecosystem where startups can thrive and grow together. By actively participating in peer networks and communities, startups can expand their networks, gain valuable insights, and access new resources and opportunities.

Investors and Funding Partners:
Securing funding is often essential for startups to fuel their growth and scale their operations. Cultivating relationships with investors and funding partners requires startups to articulate their vision, demonstrate their value proposition, and build trust and credibility. Startups should actively engage with potential investors, attend networking events and pitch competitions, and leverage their existing networks to identify funding opportunities. Building rapport with investors involves transparent communication, responsiveness to inquiries, and a compelling business case that showcases the startup's potential for success. By cultivating relationships with investors and funding partners, startups can access the capital they need to execute their growth plans and achieve their milestones.

Industry Partners and Collaborators:
Forming strategic partnerships and collaborations with industry partners can provide startups with access to resources, distribution channels, and market opportunities that can accelerate their growth. Startups should identify potential partners who share complementary goals, capabilities, and target markets and explore ways to collaborate on mutually beneficial initiatives. Building strong relationships with industry partners involves understanding their needs and objectives, articulating the value proposition of collaboration, and fostering trust and alignment. By cultivating partnerships and collaborations, startups can leverage the strengths of their partners to expand their reach, access new markets, and create additional value for customers.

Cultivating a supportive network is essential for startups to navigate the challenges and seize the opportunities of the entrepreneurial journey. By building relationships with mentors, advisors, peers, investors, and industry partners, startups can tap into a wealth of knowledge, experience, and support that can accelerate their growth and success. Whether through mentorship, peer networks, investor relationships, or strategic partnerships, startups can harness the power of a supportive network to overcome obstacles, access resources, and achieve their goals. Cultivating a supportive network is not just about networking for networking's sake but about building meaningful relationships that contribute to the long-term success and sustainability of the startup.

[O]
Human Resources and Team Building

Human resources (HR) and team building are essential components of building and managing a successful business. Let's delve into each aspect:

Human Resources (HR):

Human resources management involves overseeing the people-related aspects of a business, including recruitment, hiring, training, performance management, and employee relations. Here's a breakdown of the key functions of HR:

- **Recruitment and Hiring:** HR professionals are responsible for attracting, sourcing, and selecting qualified candidates to fill vacant positions within the organization. This involves creating job postings, screening resumes, conducting interviews, and making hiring decisions.

- **Onboarding and Orientation:** Once new employees are hired, HR facilitates the onboarding process to help them acclimate to their roles, the company culture, and the organization's policies and procedures. This includes providing necessary training and resources to set new hires up for success.

- **Training and Development:** HR oversees training and development programs to enhance employee skills, knowledge, and performance. This may involve organizing workshops, seminars, online courses, and other learning opportunities to support employee growth and career advancement.

- **Performance Management:** HR implements performance evaluation systems to assess employee performance, provide feedback, and set performance goals. This helps identify areas for improvement, recognize achievements, and align individual performance with organizational objectives.

- **Employee Relations:** HR plays a key role in managing employee relations and resolving workplace conflicts or issues. HR professionals serve as advocates for employees, ensuring fair treatment and adherence to employment laws and regulations.

- **Benefits Administration:** HR administers employee benefits programs, such as health insurance, retirement plans, and paid time off. They help employees understand their benefits options, enroll in plans, and address any benefits-related questions or concerns.

- **Compliance and Legal Responsibilities:** HR ensures compliance with labor laws, regulations, and employment standards to mitigate legal risks and maintain a safe and fair workplace environment. This includes staying up-to-date on relevant legislation and implementing policies and procedures to ensure legal compliance.

Importance of Human Resources:
Effective HR management is critical for the success and sustainability of a business for several reasons:

✓ **Talent Acquisition:**
HR helps attract and retain top talent by implementing effective recruitment and hiring strategies that align with the company's goals and culture.

✓ **Employee Development:**

HR supports employee growth and development through training and development initiatives that enhance skills, knowledge, and job satisfaction.

✓ **Performance Optimization:**

HR facilitates performance management processes that align individual and team performance with organizational objectives, driving productivity and success.

✓ **Employee Engagement:**

HR fosters a positive work environment and promotes employee engagement, morale, and satisfaction, leading to higher levels of employee retention and loyalty.

✓ **Compliance and Risk Management:**

HR ensures compliance with labor laws and regulations, minimizing legal risks and liabilities associated with employment practices.

✓ **Organizational Culture:**

HR plays a key role in shaping and maintaining the organizational culture, values, and norms that define the workplace environment and influence employee behavior and performance.

Overall, effective HR management contributes to the overall success, growth, and sustainability of a business by optimizing talent management, fostering employee development and engagement, ensuring legal compliance, and cultivating a positive organizational culture.

Now, let's explore the concept of team building:

Team Building:

Team building refers to activities and strategies aimed at improving the effectiveness, cohesion, and collaboration of a group of individuals working together toward a common goal. Team building activities can take various forms, including workshops, retreats, team-building exercises, and collaborative projects. Here's a closer look at the importance of team building:

- **Enhanced Communication:**
  Team building activities encourage open communication among team members, fostering trust and transparency. Improved communication leads to better collaboration, problem-solving, and decision-making within the team.

- **Increased Trust and Cooperation:**
  Team building fosters trust and cooperation among team members, as they learn to rely on and support each other to achieve shared objectives. Trusting relationships enable teams to work more effectively, resolve conflicts constructively, and overcome challenges together.

- **Improved Morale and Motivation:**
  Engaging in team building activities boosts morale and motivation among team members, creating a positive and supportive work environment. Feeling valued and appreciated as part of a cohesive team enhances job satisfaction and productivity.

- **Enhanced Creativity and Innovation:**
  Team building encourages creativity and innovation by providing opportunities for brainstorming, problem-solving, and exploring new ideas collaboratively. Diverse perspectives and

experiences within the team can lead to innovative solutions and approaches to challenges.

- **Strengthened Team Dynamics:**
Team building activities help identify and address strengths, weaknesses, and dynamics within the team, allowing members to understand each other's roles, preferences, and working styles better. This leads to improved team cohesion, synergy, and performance.

- **Increased Productivity and Efficiency:**
Effective team building results in more productive and efficient teams, as members are better aligned, motivated, and equipped to work together toward common goals. Teams that function cohesively can accomplish tasks more quickly and effectively than individual efforts.

- **Boosted Employee Retention:**
Team building contributes to employee satisfaction and engagement, reducing turnover and increasing employee retention rates. Employees who feel connected to their team and organization are more likely to remain committed and loyal over the long term.

- **Positive Organizational Culture:**
Team building contributes to the development of a positive organizational culture characterized by collaboration, mutual respect, and shared values. A strong team culture attracts and retains top talent, fosters innovation, and contributes to organizational success.

Overall, team building is essential for fostering effective teamwork, improving communication and collaboration, boosting morale and motivation, enhancing creativity and innovation, strengthening team dynamics, increasing productivity and efficiency, retaining top talent, and building a positive organizational culture.

By investing in team building activities and strategies, businesses can create high-performing teams that are better equipped to tackle challenges, achieve goals, and drive success in today's dynamic and competitive business environment.

[P]
Technology and IT Infrastructure:

Technology and IT infrastructure encompass the hardware, software, networks, and systems that support the operations and functions of a business. In today's digital age, technology plays a crucial role in driving efficiency, productivity, innovation, and competitiveness across all industries. Here's a closer look at the importance of technology and IT infrastructure for startups:

Operational Efficiency:

Technology enables startups to streamline their operations, automate repetitive tasks, and optimize workflows, leading to improved efficiency and productivity. By leveraging technology solutions such as cloud-based software, project management tools, and collaboration platforms, startups can maximize resource utilization and minimize manual effort.

Scalability:

Scalable technology infrastructure allows startups to grow and expand their operations without significant disruptions or constraints. Cloud computing, for example, provides scalable resources and on-demand access to computing power, storage, and applications, enabling startups to scale their IT infrastructure in line with their business needs and growth trajectory.

Data Management and Analytics:

Technology facilitates data collection, storage, analysis, and interpretation, enabling startups to derive valuable insights and make data-driven decisions. By leveraging analytics tools and business intelligence software, startups can gain a deeper understanding of their customers, market trends, and business performance, enabling them to identify opportunities, mitigate risks, and optimize strategies.

Customer Engagement and Experience:
Technology plays a key role in enhancing customer engagement and experience through digital channels such as websites, mobile apps, social media, and online customer support. Startups can leverage technology solutions such as customer relationship management (CRM) software, marketing automation platforms, and personalized messaging tools to deliver targeted, personalized, and seamless experiences to their customers.

Innovation and Differentiation:
Technology empowers startups to innovate and differentiate themselves in the market by developing unique products, services, and business models. By embracing emerging technologies such as artificial intelligence (AI), Internet of Things (IoT), blockchain, and augmented reality (AR), startups can disrupt traditional industries, create new markets, and gain a competitive edge.

Security and Compliance:
Technology infrastructure must prioritize security and compliance to protect sensitive data, mitigate cyber threats, and ensure regulatory compliance. Startups should implement robust cybersecurity measures, such as firewalls, encryption, multi-factor authentication, and regular security audits, to safeguard their systems and information assets from unauthorized access, breaches, and data loss.

Flexibility and Adaptability:
Technology infrastructure should be flexible and adaptable to accommodate changing business requirements, market dynamics, and technological advancements. Startups should embrace agile methodologies, iterative development processes, and modular architectures to iterate quickly, pivot as needed, and respond effectively to evolving customer needs and industry trends.

Cost Optimization:

Technology enables startups to optimize costs by replacing traditional infrastructure with cloud-based services, outsourcing non-core functions, and adopting software-as-a-service (SaaS) solutions. By leveraging cost-effective technology solutions and pay-as-you-go pricing models, startups can minimize upfront capital expenditures, reduce operational costs, and improve cash flow.

Overall, technology and IT infrastructure are essential enablers of startup success, providing the foundation for operational efficiency, scalability, data-driven decision-making, customer engagement, innovation, security, compliance, flexibility, adaptability, and cost optimization. By investing in the right technology solutions and building robust IT infrastructure, startups can position themselves for growth, resilience, and competitive advantage in the digital economy.

[Q]

Supply Chain Management:

Supply chain management (SCM) involves the coordination and optimization of the flow of goods, services, information, and finances from raw material suppliers to end customers. Effective supply chain management is essential for startups to ensure the timely delivery of products or services, optimize costs, and meet customer expectations. Here's why supply chain management is important for startups:

✓ **Efficient Procurement:**

Supply chain management enables startups to source raw materials, components, and resources from reliable suppliers at competitive prices. By establishing efficient procurement processes and supplier relationships, startups can ensure a steady supply of high-quality inputs to support their operations.

✓ **Production Optimization:**

Supply chain management involves planning and managing production processes to optimize efficiency, minimize waste, and meet demand forecasts. Startups can leverage production scheduling, inventory management, and quality control techniques to streamline production operations and enhance productivity.

✓ **Inventory Management:**

Effective inventory management is crucial for startups to balance supply and demand, minimize stockouts and excess inventory, and optimize working capital. By implementing inventory tracking systems, demand forecasting models, and replenishment strategies, startups can maintain optimal inventory levels and improve cash flow.

✓ **Logistics and Distribution:**
Supply chain management encompasses the transportation, warehousing, and distribution of products or services to customers. Startups must ensure efficient logistics operations, including route optimization, freight management, and order fulfillment, to deliver products to customers in a timely and cost-effective manner.

✓ **Supplier Relationships:**
Building strong relationships with suppliers is essential for startups to ensure reliability, responsiveness, and flexibility in the supply chain. By collaborating closely with suppliers, startups can address supply chain disruptions, negotiate favorable terms, and drive continuous improvement in quality and delivery performance.

✓ **Risk Management:**
Supply chain management involves identifying, assessing, and mitigating risks that may impact the supply chain, such as supplier disruptions, demand fluctuations, transportation delays, and geopolitical events. Startups should develop risk management strategies and contingency plans to minimize the impact of disruptions and ensure business continuity.

✓ **Customer Satisfaction:**
A well-managed supply chain is essential for meeting customer expectations in terms of product quality, availability, and delivery. Startups must focus on delivering superior customer service by ensuring on-time delivery, accurate order fulfillment, and responsive customer support, thereby building trust and loyalty among customers.

✓ **Cost Optimization:**
Supply chain management plays a crucial role in controlling costs throughout the supply chain, including procurement, production, transportation, and warehousing. Startups can achieve cost savings through process efficiencies, economies of scale, supplier negotiations, and inventory optimization, thereby improving profitability and competitiveness.

Overall, supply chain management is critical for startups to build a resilient, agile, and competitive supply chain that can adapt to changing market conditions, mitigate risks, and deliver value to customers. By prioritizing supply chain management and implementing best practices, startups can optimize their operations, enhance customer satisfaction, and drive sustainable growth and success.

[R]

Customer Relationship Management (CRM):

Customer Relationship Management (CRM) refers to the practices, strategies, and technologies used by businesses to manage interactions with current and potential customers. CRM encompasses various aspects of customer engagement, including sales, marketing, customer service, and support. Here's why CRM is important for startups:

✓ **Centralized Customer Data:**

CRM systems enable startups to consolidate and organize customer data from multiple sources into a centralized database. This includes contact information, purchase history, preferences, interactions, and feedback. Having a comprehensive view of customer data allows startups to gain insights into customer behavior, preferences, and needs, enabling personalized and targeted engagement.

✓ **Improved Customer Engagement:**

CRM systems facilitate personalized and targeted communication with customers across various channels, including email, phone, social media, and chat. By segmenting customers based on their interests, preferences, and buying behavior, startups can deliver relevant and timely messages, offers, and promotions, enhancing customer engagement and loyalty.

✓ **Sales Pipeline Management:**

CRM systems help startups manage their sales pipeline more effectively by tracking leads, opportunities, and deals through various stages of the sales process. By automating sales tasks, scheduling follow-ups, and providing real-time insights into sales performance, startups can streamline their sales operations and improve sales efficiency and effectiveness.

✓ **Marketing Campaign Management:**
CRM systems support the planning, execution, and analysis of marketing campaigns by providing tools for campaign creation, audience segmentation, and performance tracking. Startups can use CRM data to identify target audiences, personalize marketing messages, and measure the effectiveness of marketing initiatives, leading to higher campaign ROI and customer acquisition.

✓ **Customer Service and Support:**
CRM systems enable startups to deliver superior customer service and support by providing a platform for managing customer inquiries, issues, and feedback. By tracking customer interactions and service history, startups can resolve customer issues more efficiently, deliver timely support, and build stronger relationships with customers.

✓ **Lead Management and Nurturing:**
CRM systems help startups capture, track, and nurture leads throughout the sales funnel. By automating lead capture, scoring, and routing processes, startups can identify high-potential leads, prioritize follow-ups, and nurture relationships with prospects over time, increasing the likelihood of conversion and sales.

✓ **Data Analytics and Insights:**
CRM systems provide startups with valuable data analytics and insights that help them understand customer behavior, identify trends, and make data-driven decisions. By analyzing CRM data, startups can uncover patterns, opportunities, and areas for improvement, enabling continuous optimization of sales, marketing, and customer service strategies.

✓ **Scalability and Growth:**
CRM systems are scalable and adaptable to accommodate the evolving needs and growth of startups. As startups expand their customer base and operations, CRM systems can scale with them, providing the flexibility and functionality needed to support growing sales, marketing, and customer service requirements.

Overall, Customer Relationship Management (CRM) is essential for startups to build and maintain strong relationships with customers, drive sales and revenue growth, enhance marketing effectiveness, deliver exceptional customer service, and support sustainable business growth and success.

Conclusion: Charting Your Path to Entrepreneurial Success

Congratulations on reaching the conclusion of this comprehensive guide on starting a business from scratch. Throughout this journey, we've explored the essential steps, strategies, and considerations necessary to navigate the entrepreneurial landscape and build a successful enterprise.

From nurturing ideas into innovation to charting your course, securing funding, and choosing the right legal structure, each chapter has provided valuable insights and practical guidance to help you lay the groundwork for your entrepreneurial venture. We've delved into the intricacies of financing options, location selection, branding, and operational management, equipping you with the knowledge and tools to make informed decisions and overcome challenges along the way.

Legal and regulatory compliance, customer service excellence, effective financial management, and the cultivation of a supportive network have been emphasized as critical pillars of entrepreneurial success. By prioritizing these aspects, you can establish a strong foundation for your business and foster sustainable growth in the long term.

Furthermore, we've explored the importance of human resources and team building, technology and IT infrastructure, supply chain management, and customer relationship management in driving business success and creating value for customers. By harnessing the power of technology, leveraging efficient supply chain practices, and building strong relationships with customers, suppliers, and employees, you can position your business for competitive advantage and market leadership.

As you embark on your entrepreneurial journey, remember that entrepreneurship is not just about starting a business—it's about creating something meaningful, making a positive impact, and fulfilling your vision for the future. Stay resilient, adaptable, and open to learning from both successes and failures. Surround yourself with mentors, advisors, and a supportive network who can provide guidance, encouragement, and perspective along the way.

Ultimately, success in entrepreneurship is not guaranteed, but with passion, perseverance, and a willingness to innovate and adapt, you can overcome obstacles, seize opportunities, and chart your path to entrepreneurial success. Embrace the challenges, celebrate the victories, and never stop pursuing your dreams.

Thank you for embarking on this journey with us. We wish you all the best in your entrepreneurial endeavors, and may your business venture thrive and flourish in the dynamic and ever-evolving landscape of entrepreneurship.
